LOVING

POETRY AND ART

EDITED BY CHARLES SULLIVAN

HARRY N. ABRAMS, INC., PUBLISHERS, NEW YORK

Love is the only thing that we can carry with us when we go, and it makes the end so easy.

— Louisa May Alcott

This book is dedicated to my daughter
PAGE SULLIVAN
with pride and joy

Editor:
Margaret Rennolds Chace

Designer:
Carol Robson

Photo research, rights and reproductions:
Johanna Cypis and Catherine Ruello

On page 2: *The Birth of Venus* by Sandro Botticelli (see page 44)

Library of Congress Cataloging-in-Publication Data
Loving: poetry and art/edited by Charles Sullivan.
p. cm.
Includes index.
ISBN 0-8109-3562-7
1. Love—Poetry. 2. Love in art. I. Sullivan, Charles, 1933–
PN6110.L6L56   1992
808.81'9354—dc20   92-6517
CIP

Published in 1992 by Harry N. Abrams, Incorporated, New York
A Times Mirror Company

Printed and bound in Japan

CONTENTS

I love or have loved women of various ages, children, men both living and dead, places that I am familiar with and places that I have never seen, pets and other animals real or imaginary, several houses, one or two cars, at least two bicycles, many bits of poetry and music, a few paintings, quite a few books, an old boat of my own and five or six belonging to other people, rivers and creeks beyond number, certain hills, ridges, valleys, and trails, entire countries from time to time, and their people, the sky at night when it is packed with stars, and something that I locate vaguely out beyond the stars when I am especially scared, happy, or in need of giving thanks.

There's quite a variety—yet I can use the same two words, *love* and *loving*, to refer to my feelings about all of these things, and that seems to make sense. Although my feelings are not exactly the same in every case, they have similar elements: warmth, happiness, a kind of pride mixed with wonder, a wish to be closer to, if not to possess, the object of my feelings, a kind of generosity or protectiveness, a wish for the well-being of that object for its own sake, whether I possess it or not, and if it is a person (rather than a car or a star or some other *thing*), a desire to be loved in return.

Loving as I experience it makes me want to tell or show others what it is I love, even at the risk of losing it to them. Loving leads to celebrating love, proclaiming it in words—phone calls, letters, songs that I make up and forget (because I'm not a songwriter), or poems that I get the beginnings of, and write down, and eventually follow to the end, lifting the images and words, one by one, out of my unconscious, because I am a poet. For example:

> *In this dream*
> *I run my fingers*
> *through your hair,*

> *smoothing it,*
> *shaping it closer*
> *to your skull,*
> *tenderly, carefully,*
> *as though I were one*
> *of the sculptors, as though*
> *I had not arrived too late*
> *to help create*
> *your beauty.*

I don't have to be a poet, however, to understand and appreciate the feelings of other people who have written poetry about loving. I can share the excitement of Robert Browning, embracing Elizabeth, "two hearts beating each to each," and I can imagine how she felt when she wrote: "How do I love thee? Let me count the ways." I know what it is like to withdraw, as Yeats did, when one's love is not returned:

> *Love fled*
> *And paced upon the mountains overhead*
> *And hid his face amid a crowd of stars.*

I also know how it feels to be withdrawn from, as Sylvia Plath described it:

> *The comets*
> *Have such a space to cross,*
>
> *Such coldness, forgetfulness.*

I could fall in love with a new car, like Karl Shapiro, or feel myself being borne aloft by love, like Emily Dickinson:

> *The world did drop away*
> *As countries from the feet*
> *Of him that leaneth in balloon*
> *Upon an ether street.*

And what about you? Can you remember learning to kiss? This is how a very young poet, Brian Mueller, describes it:

> Kissing someone on the lips
> is like sharing a ripe fruit
> while dancing in the snow

Have you ever loved someone, as Theodore Roethke may have done, because they were so beautiful, and moved so beautifully?

> I knew a woman, lovely in her bones,
> When small birds sighed, she would sigh back at them;
> Ah, when she moved, she moved more ways than one:
> The shapes a bright container can contain!

Then again, have you ever *resented* being loved for such reasons, as in Barbara Angell's poem?

> This body that you love so much
> will take its turn,
> abandoned briefcase,
> lost papers, old
> sack of news.
>
> You love its fires, its ears,
> and how it moves, it moves,
> this body
> that you love so much.

When your beloved is far away, do you miss them terribly, like Rihaku? Or is there a tinge of suspicion, jealousy, such as Elizabeth Bishop suggests?

> In your next letter I wish you'd say
> Where you are going and what you are doing:
> How are the plays, and after the plays,
> What other pleasures you're pursuing.

Or does your love blaze forth, as in Louise Bogan's poem "Men Loved Wholly Beyond Wisdom"?

> Like a fire in a dry thicket,
> Rising within women's eyes
> Is the love men must return.

Most of the world's love poetry is about men loving women or women loving men. But men who love men, and women who love women, are also subjects of poetry. W. H. Auden, for example, wrote:

> Lay your sleeping head, my love,
> Human on my faithless arm;
> Time and fevers burn away
> Individual beauty from
> Thoughtful children. . . .

And what of the love between parents and children? Sylvia Plath says to her young daughter:

> One cry, and I stumble from bed, cow-heavy and floral
> In my Victorian nightgown.
> Your mouth opens clean as a cat's. . . .

Is this an emotion, or merely an instinct, an automatic response to a particular stimulus? Is there any choice involved? But then again, how much choice was involved when Romeo and Juliet fell in love?

Loving and the poetry that expresses it can be broad, sweeping, universal. Gerard Manley Hopkins gave thanks for "all things counter, original, spare, strange." Spiritual love can be found in the poetry of every culture known to us. Amenhotep IV, an Egyptian pharaoh of the fourteenth century B.C., became so devoted to Aton the sun-god that he changed his own name to Aknaton, and wrote:

> Thou art shining, beautiful, strong;
> Thy love is great and mighty,
> Thy rays are cast into every face.
> Thy glowing hue brings life to hearts,
> When thou has filled the Two Lands with thy love.

Love as a positive force, giving life (or helping us to deal with death), can also be expressed in poetry that is not obviously religious or spiritual. Erica Jong writes:

> I try to keep
> falling in love
> if only to keep
> death

at bay. . . .

love drives
the poem—

& the poem
is
hope.

Hope for what? Not for a painless, deathless existence, but for the chance to love and be loved (again or still), in spite of pain and death. "Though lovers be lost," said Dylan Thomas, "love shall not." Why not? Because there will always be people, according to the poet's view, and so there will always be love:

> *And death shall have no dominion.*
> *No more may gulls cry at their ears*
> *Or waves break loud on the seashores;*
> *Where blew a flower may a flower no more*
> *Lift its head to the blows of the rain;*
> *Though they be mad and dead as nails,*
> *Heads of the characters hammer through daisies;*
> *Break in the sun till the sun breaks down,*
> *And death shall have no dominion.*

Often the great poetry is so intensely visual that we can see things vividly through verbal images, whether these things be real and immediate (a flower lifting its head to the blows of the rain) or imaginary and remote (the sun breaking down). One poet in particular, Archibald MacLeish, has made this point dramatically clear. Having challenged Shakespeare, no less, as to whether words alone can make the loved one immortal, MacLeish concludes his poem with a vivid demonstration of what words alone *can* do:

> *I will say you were young and straight and your skin*
> *   fair*
> *And you stood in the door and the sun was a shadow of*
> *   leaves on your shoulders*
> *And a leaf on your hair—*
> *   I will not speak of the famous beauty of dead*
> *   women:*

> *I will say the shape of a leaf lay once on your hair.*
> *Till the world ends and the eyes are out and the*
> *   mouths broken,*
> *Look! It is there!*

And so it is.

Some poets, however, have gone further—illustrating their own work, or collaborating with artists, or writing poems about works of visual art. From the other side, many artists have illustrated poetry, sometimes in collaboration with the poet, sometimes not. Often the results of these efforts *enhance* both the verbal images and the visual images; we see things differently, we find new meanings or further possibilities to explore. Occasionally the enhancement is so great that we seem to be dealing with a new work of art: a whole that is different from the sum of its parts.

The idea of *editorially* combining poetry with art is more recent, and more risky; the selections and combinations are usually made by someone other than the people who wrote the poems, painted the pictures, and so on. If the "someone" is a team or a committee, the resulting book may reflect a mixture of tastes. If it is an individual (like me) then my taste, my likes and dislikes, my judgment will largely determine what is left out, what is put in, and what goes with what.

In several previous books, starting with *America in Poetry* (Abrams, 1988), I have developed a theme or a series of themes through combinations of poetry and art (including paintings, drawings, photographs, and other works). There is no precise technique for doing so. My approach is to identify many possibilities and to move back and forth among them many times, until I begin to see the possible poetry as a whole, the possible art as a whole. Gradually some specific patterns or combinations emerge. But there may be times when I have a sense of missing ingredients, and no sure method of finding them. Sometimes the search is long and frustrating; other times, I can almost reach out my hand and immediately locate what I need.

Working on this book, for example, I came across the wonderful MacLeish poem, "'Not Marble, Nor the Gilded Monuments,'" at the outset. After that I quickly remembered the Shakespeare sonnet from which its title comes. It took me a while longer to select the *Venus de Milo* to go with the Shakespeare. But then the discovery of Clarence White's photograph *Girl with a Venus*, to accompany the MacLeish poem, was pure serendipity—I happened to be browsing through a pile of secondhand books for an entirely different project. The resulting combinations work beautifully for me; I hope they do for you, too.

This book is organized into eleven sections, which I call: the poet's view, legendary lovers, seeking beauty, first love, heart to heart, husband and wife, hidden feelings, parents and children, love of creation, spiritual love, and the state of the heart. Each of these sections represents a theme that I have found in poetry and art. Within each section, the contents vary to reflect different points of view. There is little repetition, but there are many variations on the several themes.

Some of the poets and some of the artists included here are famous, or at least familiar; others are unfamiliar, even unknown to most people. This mixture is intentional. Considering "first love," for example, we need to know how Elizabeth Barrett Browning and Pierre-Auguste Renoir have portrayed the heights of romance, but we also need to know how first love has been seen by Brian Mueller, a seventh grader in Chico, California, when he wrote "Kissing."

Another interesting feature of this book is the creation of "dialogues" among two or more poets who have dealt with similar themes but from different perspectives. For example, the book begins with a group of three poems about love as the poet sees it. Dylan Thomas works late at night, writing not to express his own thoughts and feelings,

> But for the lovers, their arms
> Round the griefs of the ages,
> Who pay no praise or wages
> Nor heed my craft or art.

Pablo Neruda, also working late at night, can think and write only of the woman he has lost—nobody else:

> What does it matter that my love could not keep her.
> The night is shattered and she is not with me.

Anna Akhmatova has lost a lover, too, but her feelings and her poetry are quite different from Neruda's:

> I swear by the miracle-working ikon,
> and by the fire and smoke of our nights:
> I will never come back to you.

Loving, then, may be somewhat different and distinct for each of us, yet we all participate in the same or similar feelings, one way or another. So we can share what has been thought and said about it, and what has been shown visually, even as we learn to go beyond the limits of our own experience, beyond the everyday boundaries of language and culture, distance and time, into the realm that may be most truly universal.

CHARLES SULLIVAN
WASHINGTON, D.C.

9

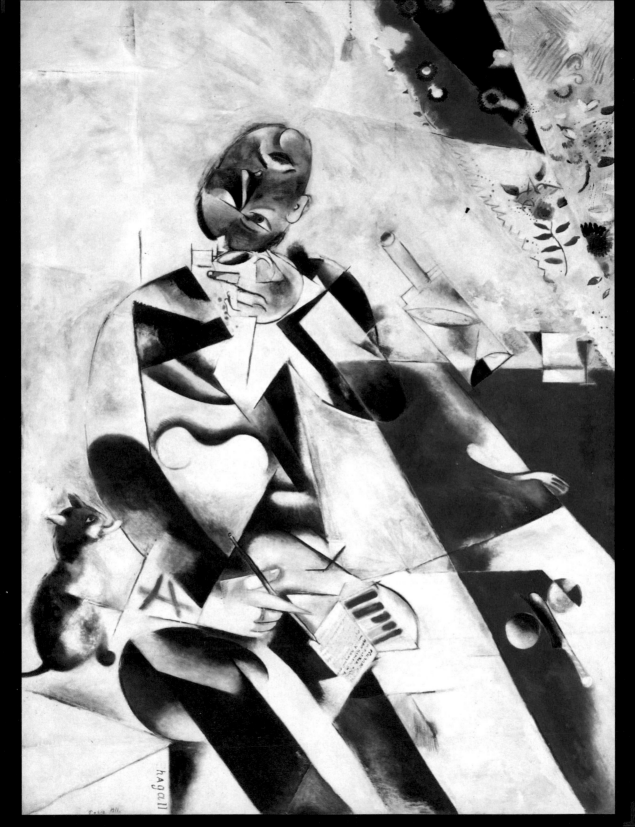

IN MY CRAFT OR SULLEN ART

Dylan Thomas

In my craft or sullen art
Exercised in the still night
When only the moon rages
And the lovers lie abed
With all their griefs in their arms,
I labour by singing light
Not for ambition or bread
Or the strut or trade of charms
On the ivory stages
But for the common wages
Of their most secret heart.

Not for the proud man apart
From the raging moon I write
On these spindrift pages
Nor for the towering dead
With their nightingales and psalms
But for the lovers, their arms
Round the griefs of the ages,
Who pay no praise or wages
Nor heed my craft or art.

Half Past Three (The Poet) by Marc Chagall. 1911.
Oil on canvas, 77½ x 57½".
Philadelphia Museum of Art:
Louise and Walter Arensberg Collection

YOU THOUGHT I WAS THAT TYPE

Anna Akhmatova

TRANSLATED FROM RUSSIAN BY RICHARD MCKANE

You thought I was that type:
that you could forget me,
and that I'd plead and weep and throw myself
under the hooves of a bay mare,

or that I'd ask the sorcerers
for some magic potion made from roots
and send you a terrible gift:
my precious perfumed handkerchief.

Damn you! I will not grant
your cursed soul vicarious tears or a single glance.
And I swear to you by the garden of the angels,
I swear by the miracle-working ikon,
and by the fire and smoke of our nights:
I will never come back to you.

TONIGHT I CAN WRITE THE SADDEST LINES

Pablo Neruda

TRANSLATED FROM SPANISH BY W. S. MERWIN

Tonight I can write the saddest lines.

Write, for example, "The night is shattered
and the blue stars shiver in the distance."

The night wind revolves in the sky and sings.

Tonight I can write the saddest lines.
I loved her, and sometimes she loved me too.

Through nights like this one I held her in my arms.
I kissed her again and again under the endless sky.

She loved me, sometimes I loved her too.
How could one not have loved her great still eyes.

Tonight I can write the saddest lines.
To think that I do not have her. To feel that I have lost her.

To hear the immense night, still more immense without her.
And the verse falls to the soul like dew to the pasture.

What does it matter that my love could not keep her.
The night is shattered and she is not with me.

This is all. In the distance someone is singing. In the distance.
My soul is not satisfied that it has lost her.

My sight searches for her as though to go to her.
My heart looks for her, and she is not with me.

The same night whitening the same trees.
We, of that time, are no longer the same.

I no longer love her, that's certain, but how I loved her.
My voice tried to find the wind to touch her hearing.

Another's. She will be another's. Like my kisses before.
Her voice. Her bright body. Her infinite eyes.

I no longer love her, that's certain, but maybe I love her.
Love is so short, forgetting is so long.

Because through nights like this one I held her in my arms
my soul is not satisfied that it has lost her.

Though this be the last pain that she makes me suffer
and these the last verses that I write for her.

The Fall of Man and *The Expulsion from the Garden of Eden* by Michelangelo. 1508–12. Fresco, from the ceiling of the Sistine Chapel, The Vatican, Rome

A LITTLE KNOWLEDGE
The Book of Genesis 3:22–24
THE BIBLE ACCORDING TO THE MASORETIC TEXT

And the Lord God said: "Behold, the man is become as one of us, to know good and evil; and now, lest he put forth his hand, and take also of the tree of life, and eat, and live for ever." Therefore the Lord God sent him forth from the garden of Eden, to till the ground from whence he was taken. So He drove out the man; and He placed at the east of the garden of Eden the cherubim, and the flaming sword which turned every way, to keep the way to the tree of life.

A PITY—WE WERE SUCH A GOOD INVENTION

Yehuda Amichai

TRANSLATED FROM HEBREW BY ASSIA GUTMANN

They amputated
Your thighs off my hips.
As far as I'm concerned
They are all surgeons. All of them.

They dismantled us
Each from the other.
As far as I'm concerned
They are all engineers. All of them.

A pity. We were such a good
And loving invention.
An aeroplane made from a man and wife.
Wings and everything.
We hovered a little above the earth.

We even flew a little.

THE NIGHT DANCES

Sylvia Plath

A smile fell in the grass.
Irretrievable!

And how will your night dances
Lose themselves. In mathematics?

Such pure leaps and spirals—
Surely they travel

The world forever, I shall not entirely
Sit emptied of beauties, the gift

Of your small breath, the drenched grass
Smell of your sleeps, lilies, lilies.

Their flesh bears no relation.
Cold folds of ego, the calla,

And the tiger, embellishing itself—
Spots, and a spread of hot petals.

The comets
Have such a space to cross,

Such coldness, forgetfulness.
So your gestures flake off—

Warm and human, then their pink light
Bleeding and peeling

Through the black amnesias of heaven.
Why am I given

These lamps, these planets
Falling like blessings, like flakes

Six-sided, white
On my eyes, my lips, my hair

Touching and melting.
Nowhere.

LOVESONG
Ted Hughes

He loved her and she loved him
His kisses sucked out her whole past and future
    or tried to
He had no other appetite
She bit him she gnawed him she sucked
She wanted him complete inside her
Safe and sure forever and ever
Their little cries fluttered into the curtains

Her eyes wanted nothing to get away
Her looks nailed down his hands his wrists
    his elbows
He gripped her hard so that life
Should not drag her from that moment
He wanted all future to cease
He wanted to topple with his arms round her
Off that moment's brink and into nothing
Or everlasting or whatever there was
Her embrace was an immense press
To print him into her bones
His smiles were the garrets of a fairy palace
Where the real world would never come
Her smiles were spider bites
So he would lie still till she felt hungry
His words were occupying armies
Her laughs were an assassin's attempts
His looks were bullets daggers of revenge
Her glances were ghosts in the corner with
    horrible secrets
His whispers were whips and jackboots
Her kisses were lawyers steadily writing
His caresses were the last hooks of a castaway
Her love-tricks were the grinding of locks

And their deep cries crawled over the floors
Like an animal dragging a great trap
His promises were the surgeon's gag
Her promises took the top off his skull
She would get a brooch made of it
His vows pulled out all her sinews
He showed her how to make a love-knot
Her vows put his eyes in formalin
At the back of her secret drawer
Their screams stuck in the wall

Their heads fell apart into sleep like the two
    halves
Of a lopped melon, but love is hard to stop

In their entwined sleep they exchanged arms
    and legs
In their dreams their brains took each other
    hostage

In the morning they wore each other's face

THE POINT OF DEATH
FROM *Romeo and Juliet*
William Shakespeare

How oft when men are at the point of death
Have they been merry! which their keepers call
A lightning before death: O! how may I
Call this a lightning? O my love! my wife!
Death, that hath suck'd the honey of thy breath,
Hath had no power yet upon thy beauty:
Thou art not conquer'd; beauty's ensign yet
Is crimson in thy lips and in thy cheeks,
And death's pale flag is not advancèd there.

Rudolf Nureyev and Margot Fonteyn in Romeo and Juliet, Royal Ballet. Photograph by Reg Wilson. 1965

WHEN I WAS FAIR AND YOUNG
AND FAVOUR GRACÈD ME

Queen Elizabeth I

When I was fair and young and favour gracèd me,
Of many was I sought, their mistress for to be:
But I did scorn them all, and answered them therefore,
    "Go, go, go, seek some other where:
           Importune me no more."

How many weeping eyes I made to pine with woe,
How many sighing hearts, I have no skill to show:
Yet I the prouder grew, and answered them therefore,
    "Go, go, go, seek some other where:
           Importune me no more."

Then spake fair Venus' son, that proud victorious boy,
And said, "Fine Dame, since that you be so coy,
I will so pluck your plumes that you shall say no more,
    'Go, go, go, seek some other where:
           Importune me no more.'"

When he had spake these words, such change grew in my breast
That neither night nor day, since that, I could take any rest:
Then lo, I did repent that I had said before,
    "Go, go, go, seek some other where:
           Importune me no more."

The Toilet of Venus (The Rokeby Venus) by Diego Velázquez. c. 1648–51. Oil on canvas, 48¼ x 69¾"
Reproduced by Courtesy of the Trustees, The National Gallery, London

A FAREWELL TO FALSE LOVE

Sir Walter Raleigh

Farewell false love, the oracle of lies,
A mortal foe and enemy to rest:
An envious boy, from whom all cares arise,
A bastard vile, a beast with rage possessed:
A way of error, a temple full of treason,
In all effects, contrary unto reason.

A poisoned serpent covered all with flowers,
Mother of sighs, and murderer of repose,
A sea of sorrows from whence are drawn such showers
As moisture lend to every grief that grows,
A school of guile, a net of deep deceit,
A gilded hook, that holds a poisoned bait.

A fortress foiled, which reason did defend,
A Siren song, a fever of the mind,
A maze wherein affection finds no end,
A ranging cloud that runs before the wind,
A substance like the shadow of the sun,
A goal of grief for which the wisest run.

A quenchless fire, a nurse of trembling fear,
A path that leads to peril and mishap,
A true retreat of sorrow and despair,
An idle boy that sleeps in pleasure's lap,
A deep mistrust of that which certain seems,
A hope of that which reason doubtful deems.

Sith then thy trains my younger years betrayed
And for my faith ingratitude I find.
And sith repentance hath my wrongs bewrayed
Whose course was ever contrary to kind.
False Love; Desire; and Beauty frail adieu
Dead is the root whence all these fancies grew.

Sir Walter Raleigh by Nicholas Hilliard. c. 1585.
Miniature. National Portrait Gallery, London

Maud Gonne.
Photograph by Tony Linck. c. 1950.
LIFE *Magazine* © Time Warner Inc.

WHEN YOU ARE OLD

W. B. Yeats

When you are old and grey and full of sleep,
And nodding by the fire, take down this book,
And slowly read, and dream of the soft look
Your eyes had once, and of their shadows deep;

How many loved your moments of glad grace,
And loved your beauty with love false or true,
But one man loved the pilgrim soul in you,
And loved the sorrows of your changing face;

And bending down beside the glowing bars,
Murmur, a little sadly, how Love fled
And paced upon the mountains overhead
And hid his face amid a crowd of stars.

Antonio Nardone, Called Cacao, Rodin's Model. Musée Rodin.
Photograph by Jean Mounicq. 1959

The Kiss by Auguste Rodin. 1886–98.
Marble, over lifesize. Musée Rodin, Paris

GROW OLD ALONG WITH ME
Robert Browning

Grow old along with me!
The best is yet to be,
The last of life, for which the first was made:
Our times are in his hand
Who saith 'a whole I planned,
Youth shows but half: trust God: see all
   nor be afraid!

Yoko Ono and John Lennon. Photograph by Kishin Shinoyama. 1980

GROW OLD WITH ME

John Lennon

Grow old along with me
The best is yet to be
When our time has come
We will be as one
God bless our love
God bless our love

LET ME COUNT THE WAYS

Yoko Ono

Let me count the ways how I love you
It's like that gentle wind you feel at dawn
It's like that first sun that hits the dew
It's like that cloud with a gold lining telling us softly
That it'll be a good day, a good day for us
Thank you, thank you, thank you

HOW DO I LOVE THEE?
LET ME COUNT THE WAYS

Elizabeth Barrett Browning

How do I love thee? Let me count the ways.
I love thee to the depth and breadth and height
My soul can reach, when feeling out of sight
For the ends of being and ideal grace,
I love thee to the level of everyday's
Most quiet need, by sun and candle-light.
I love thee freely, as men strive for right:
I love thee purely, as they turn from praise.
I love thee with the passion put to use
In my old griefs, and with my childhood's faith.
I love thee with a love I seemed to lose
With my lost saints,—I love thee with the breath,
Smiles, tears, of all my life!—And, if God choose,
I shall but love thee better after death.

Blue and Gold: The Rose Azalea
by James McNeill Whistler.
c. 1890–95. Watercolor on brown paper,
10⅞ x 7⅛". Courtesy of the Freer Gallery of Art,
Smithsonian Institution, Washington, D.C. (94.25)

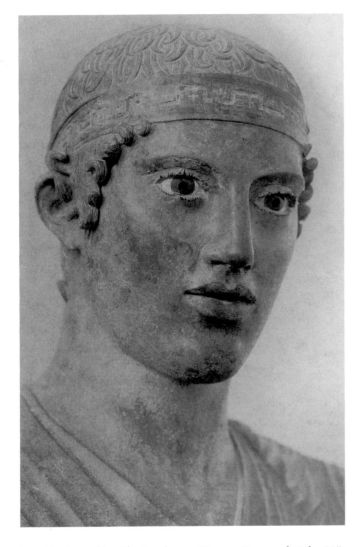

The Charioteer (detail). Greek, c. 477 B.C. Bronze, height 71".
Archeological Museum, Delphi

I DIED FOR BEAUTY

Emily Dickinson

I died for Beauty—but was scarce
Adjusted in the Tomb
When One who died for Truth, was lain
In an adjoining Room—

He questioned softly "Why I failed"?
"For Beauty", I replied—
"And I—for Truth—Themself are One—
We Brethren, are", He said—

And so, as Kinsmen, met a Night—
We talked between the Rooms—
Until the Moss had reached our lips—
And covered up—our names—

Fragment of a Grave Stele. Greek, c. 560 B.C. Marble. National Museum, Athens

WAS THIS THE FACE

Christopher Marlowe

Was this the face that launched a thousand ships
And burnt the topless towers of Ilium?
Sweet Helen, make me immortal with a kiss.
Her lips suck forth my soul; see where it flies!—
Come, Helen, come, give me my soul again.
Here will I dwell, for Heaven is in these lips.
And all is dross that is not Helena.
I will be Paris, and for love of thee,
Instead of Troy, shall Wertenberg be sacked:
And I will combat with weak Menelaus,

And wear thy colours on my plumèd crest:
Yea, I will wound Achilles in the heel,
And then return to Helen for a kiss.
Oh, thou art fairer than the evening air
Clad in the beauty of a thousand stars;
Brighter art thou than flaming Jupiter
When he appeared to hapless Semele:
More lovely than the monarch of the sky
In wanton Arethusa's azured arms:
And none but thee shall be my paramour.

HELEN
H. D. (Hilda Doolittle)

All Greece hates
the still eyes in the white face,
the lustre as of olives
where she stands,
and the white hands.

All Greece reviles
the wan face when she smiles,
hating it deeper still
when it grows wan and white,
remembering past enchantments
and past ills.

Greece sees, unmoved,
God's daughter, born of love,
the beauty of cool feet
and slenderest knees,
could love indeed the maid,
only if she were laid,
white ash amid funereal cypresses.

H. D. (Hilda Doolittle). Photograph by Man Ray. c. 1922

NOT MARBLE, NOR THE GILDED MONUMENTS

William Shakespeare

Not marble, nor the gilded monuments
Of princes shall outlive this powerful rhyme;
But you shall shine more bright in these contents
Than unswept stone besmeared with sluttish time.
When wasteful war shall statues overturn,
And broils root out the work of masonry,
Not Mars his sword nor war's quick fire shall burn
The living record of your memory.
'Gainst death and all oblivious enmity
Shall you pace forth: your praise shall still find room
Even in the eyes of all posterity
That wear this world out to the ending doom.
     So, till the judgement that yourself arise,
     You live in this, and dwell in lovers' eyes.

Venus de Milo.
Greek, c. 100 B.C.
Marble, height 6'10".
Louvre, Paris

Girl with a Venus. Photograph by Clarence H. White. c. 1900. The Library of Congress

"NOT MARBLE, NOR THE GILDED MONUMENTS"
Archibald MacLeish

The praisers of women in their proud and beautiful poems,
Naming the grave and the hair and the eyes,
Boasted those they loved should be forever remembered:
These were lies.

The words sound but the face in the Istrian sun is forgotten.
The poet speaks but to her dead ears no more.
The sleek throat is gone—and the breast that was troubled to listen:
Shadow from door.

Therefore I will not praise your knees nor your fine walking
Telling you men shall remember your name as long
As lips move or breath is spent or the iron of English
Rings from a tongue.

I shall say you were young, and your arms straight, and your mouth scarlet:
I shall say you will die and none will remember you:
Your arms change, and none remember the swish of your garments,
Nor the click of your shoe.

Not with my hand's strength, not with difficult labor
Springing the obstinate words to the bones of your breast
And the stubborn line to your young stride and the breath to your breathing
And the beat to your haste
Shall I prevail on the hearts of unborn men to remember.

(What is a dead girl but a shadowy ghost
Or a dead man's voice but a distant and vain affirmation
Like dream words most)

Therefore I will not speak of the undying glory of women.
I will say you were young and straight and your skin fair
And you stood in the door and the sun was a shadow of leaves on your shoulders
And a leaf on your hair—
   I will not speak of the famous beauty of dead women:
   I will say the shape of a leaf lay once on your hair.
   Till the world ends and the eyes are out and the mouths broken,
   Look! It is there!

Anne by Alex Katz. 1973. Color lithograph, 27 x 36". Courtesy Brooke Alexander, New York

LOVE IS NOT BLIND. I SEE WITH SINGLE EYE
Edna St. Vincent Millay

Love is not blind. I see with single eye
Your ugliness and other women's grace.
I know the imperfection of your face,—
The eyes too wide apart, the brow too high
For beauty. Learned from earliest youth am I
In loveliness, and cannot so erase
Its letters from my mind, that I may trace
You faultless, I must love until I die.
More subtle is the sovereignty of love:
So am I caught that when I say, "Not fair,"
'Tis but as if I said, "Not here—not there—
Not risen—not writing letters." Well I know
What is this beauty men are babbling of;
I wonder only why they prize it so.

THE LOVER MOURNS FOR THE LOSS OF LOVE
W. B. Yeats

Pale brows, still hands and dim hair,
I had a beautiful friend
And dreamed that the old despair
Would end in love in the end:
She looked in my heart one day
And saw your image was there;
She has gone weeping away.

Kiss Me. Photograph by Hugh Bell. c. 1975

Gregory by David Hockney. 1979.
Ink on paper, 30 x 22". Courtesy of the Artist.
© David Hockney

BLACK WOMAN
Naomi Long Madgett

My hair is springy like the forest grasses
that cushion the feet of squirrels—
crinkled and blown in a south breeze
like the small leaves of native bushes.

My black eyes are coals burning
like a low, full jungle moon
through the darkness of being.
In a clear pool I see my face,
know my knowing.

My hands move pianissimo
over the music of the night:
gentle birds fluttering through leaves and grasses
they have not always loved,
nesting, finding home.

Where are my lovers?
Where are my tall, my lovely princes
dancing in slow grace
toward knowledge of my beauty?
Where
are my beautiful
black men?

THE MIRROR
Louise Glück

Watching you in the mirror I wonder
what it is like to be so beautiful
and why you do not love
but cut yourself, shaving
like a blind man. I think you let me stare
so you can turn against yourself
with greater violence,
needing to show me how you scrape the flesh away
scornfully and without hesitation
until I see you correctly,
as a man bleeding, not
the reflection I desire.

A Lady in Waiting, detail from *The Arrival of Bathsheba at the Palace of David*. Brussels, c. 1510–20. Tapestry. Musée National de la Renaissance, Chateau d'Ecouen, Val d'Oise, France

THEY FLEE FROM ME
THAT SOMETIME DID ME SEEK
Sir Thomas Wyatt

They fle from me that sometyme did me seke
    With naked fote stalking in my chambre.
I have sene theim gentill tame and meke
    That nowe are wyld and do not remembre
    That sometyme they put theimself in daunger
To take bred at my hand; and nowe they raunge
Besely seking with a continuell chaunge.

Thancked be fortune, it hath ben othrewise
    Twenty tymes better; but ons in speciall,
In thyn arraye after a pleasaunt gyse,
    When her lose gowne from her shoulders
      did fall,
    And she me caught in her armes long
      and small;
Therewithall swetely did me kysse,
And softely saide, *dere hert, howe like you this?*

It was no dreme: I lay brode waking.
    But all is torned thorough my gentilnes
Into a straunge fasshion of forsaking;
    And I have leve to goo of her goodenes,
    And she also to vse new fangilnes.
But syns that I so kyndely ame serued,
I would fain knowe what she hath deserued.

Afghan Refugee. Photograph by Steve McCurry. 1984

THE MIRAGE

Avedik Issahakian
TRANSLATED FROM ARMENIAN
BY DIANA DER HOVANESSIAN

One day in the desert a bedouin
looked up and saw a mirage shimmering
ahead. Not water, but the splendor
of a dazzling girl.

In the thirsty, burning desert
among dry thorns, under a shadowless sun
he tried to reach her but instead
of that marvelous love he found death.

In his immaterial, immortal sleep
he still saw the splendor of that girl
shimmering ahead, an eternal mirage.
And in his endless dream he began to walk
looking for her.

THE FIRST DAY

Christina Rossetti

I wish I could remember the first day,
First hour, first moment of your meeting me;
If bright or dim the season, it might be
Summer or winter for aught I can say.
So unrecorded did it slip away,
So blind was I to see and to foresee,
So dull to mark the budding of my tree
That would not blossom yet for many a May.
If only I could recollect it! Such
A day of days! I let it come and go
As traceless as a thaw of bygone snow.
It seemed to mean so little, meant so much!
If only now I could recall that touch,
First touch of hand in hand!—Did one but know!

Oinochoe from Tomb L at Arkades (detail),
Crete. 675–640 B.C. Clay.
Herakleion Archaeological Museum, Crete

41

AT BAIA

H. D. (Hilda Doolittle)

I should have thought
In a dream you would have brought
Some lovely perilous thing,
Orchids piled in a great sheath,
As who would say (in a dream)
I send you this,
Who left the blue veins
Of your throat unkissed.

Why was it that your hands
(That never took mine)
Your hands that I could see
Drift over the orchid heads
So carefully,
Your hands, so fragile, sure to lift,
So gently, the fragile flower stuff—
Ah, ah, how was it

You never sent (in a dream)
The very form, the very scent,
Not heavy, not sensuous,
But perilous—perilous—
Of orchids, piled in a great sheath,
And folded underneath on a bright scroll
Some word:

Flower sent to flower;
For white hands, the lesser white,
Less lovely of flower leaf,

Or

Lover to lover, no kiss,
No touch, but forever and ever this.

Adam and Eve by Francis Picabia.
1941–43. Oil on wood, 41 x 29¼".
Collection: Emily and Jerry Spiegel, Kings Point, New York

The Birth of Venus by Sandro Botticelli. c. 1480. Tempera on canvas, 5' 8⅞" x 9' 1⅞". Galleria degli Uffizi, Florence

THE BAIT

John Donne

Come live with me and be my love,
And we will some new pleasures prove
Of golden sands and crystal brooks,
With silken lines and silver hooks.

There will the river whispering run,
Warm'd by thine eyes more than the sun,
And there th'enamor'd fish will stay,
Begging themselves they may betray.

When thou wilt swim in that live bath,
Each fish which every channel hath
Will amorously to thee swim,
Gladder to catch thee than thou him.

If thou to be so seen be'st loath,
By sun or moon, thou dark'nest both,
And if myself have leave to see,
I need not their light, having thee.

Let others freeze with angling reeds,
And cut their legs with shells and weeds,
Or treacherously poor fish beset
With strangling snare or windowy net;

Let coarse bold hands from slimy nest
The bedded fish in banks outwrest,
Or curious traitors, sleave–silk flies,
Bewitch poor fishes' wand'ring eyes.

For thee, thou need'st no such deceit,
For thou theyself art thine own bait;
That fish that is not catch'd thereby,
Alas, is wiser far than I.

THE LADY'S "YES"

Elizabeth Barrett Browning

"Yes," I answered you last night;
　"No," this morning, sir, I say:
Colors seen by candle–light
　Will not look the same by day.

When the viols played their best,
　Lamps above, and laughs below,
Love me sounded like a jest,
　Fit for *yes* or fit for *no*.

Call me false or call me free,
　Vow, whatever light may shine,—
No man on your face shall see
　Any grief for change on mine.

Yet the sin is on us both;
　Time to dance is not to woo;
Wooing light makes fickle troth,
　Scorn of *me* recoils on *you*.

Learn to win a lady's faith
　Nobly, as the thing is high,
Bravely, as for life and death,
　With a loyal gravity.

Lead her from the festive boards,
　Point her to the starry skies,
Guard her, by your truthful words,
　Pure from courtship's flatteries.

By your truth she shall be true,
　Ever true, as wives of yore;
And her *yes*, once said for you,
　SHALL be Yes for evermore.

The Dance at Bougival by Pierre–Auguste Renoir. 1883. Oil on canvas,
71⅛ x 38⅝". Courtesy, Museum of Fine Arts, Boston. Picture Fund

IT WAS A QUIET WAY

Emily Dickinson

It was a quiet way
He asked if I was his.
I made no answer of the tongue
But answer of the eyes.

And then he bore me high
Before this mortal noise,
With swiftness as of chariots
And distance as of wheels.

The world did drop away
As countries from the feet
Of him that leaneth in balloon
Upon an ether street.

The gulf behind was not—
The continents were new.
Eternity it was—before
Eternity was due.

No seasons were to us—
It was not night nor noon,
For sunrise stopped upon the place
And fastened it in dawn.

Aurora, attributed to Betsy C. Lathrop. c. 1815.
Watercolor and gold paper collage on silk, 18¼ x 18¼".
Abby Aldrich Rockefeller Folk Art Center, Williamsburg, Virginia

LOVE

Takasaki Masakaze

TRANSLATED FROM JAPANESE BY MIYAMORI ASATARO

Oh, never before have I known, among
    All my heart's sentiments,
 One that was hard for me to confide
    To my own parents.

Lovers on a Balcony by Utamaro. 1788. Oban color-printed album plate from *The Poem of the Pillow.*
Reproduced by Courtesy of the Trustees of the British Museum, London

William Butler Yeats at Lennox Robinson's Cottage. Photograph by S. J. McCormack. c.1933.
Robert W. Woodruff Library, Special Collections, Emory University, Atlanta

BROWN PENNY

W. B. Yeats

I whispered, "I am too young,"
And then, "I am old enough";
Wherefore I threw a penny
To find out if I might love.
"Go and love, go and love, young man,
If the lady be young and fair."
Ah, penny, brown penny, brown penny,
I am looped in the loops of her hair.

O love is the crooked thing,
There is nobody wise enough
To find out all that is in it,
For he would be thinking of love
Till the stars had run away
And the shadows eaten the moon.
Ah, penny, brown penny, brown penny,
One cannot begin it too soon.

50

The Bride of the Wind by Oskar Kokoschka. 1914. Oil on canvas, 71¼ x 87".
Oeffentliche Kunstsammlung, Basel, Kunstmuseum, Switzerland

MEETING AT NIGHT

Robert Browning

The grey sea and the long black land;
And the yellow half-moon large and low;
And the startled little waves that leap
In fiery ringlets from their sleep,
As I gain the cove with pushing prow,
And quench its speed i' the slushy sand.

Then a mile of warm sea-scented beach;
Three fields to cross till a farm appears;
A tap at the pane, the quick sharp scratch
And blue spurt of a lighted match,
And a voice less loud, through its joys and fears,
Than the two hearts beating each to each!

WILD NIGHTS

Emily Dickinson

Wild Nights—Wild Nights!
Were I with thee
Wild Nights should be
Our luxury!

Futile—the Winds—
To a Heart in port—
Done with the Compass—
Done with the Chart!

Rowing in Eden—
Ah, the Sea!
Might I but moor—Tonight—
In Thee!

COUNTING THE BEATS

Robert Graves

You, love, and I,
(He whispers) you and I,
And if no more than only you and I,
What care you or I?

Counting the beats,
Counting the slow heart beats,
The bleeding to death of time in slow heart beats,
Wakeful they lie.

Cloudless day,
Night, and a cloudless day,
Yet the huge storm will burst upon their heads one day
From a bitter sky.

Where shall we be,
(She whispers) where shall we be,
When death strikes home, O where then shall we be
Who were you and I?

Not there but here,
(He whispers) only here,
As we are, here, together, now and here,
Always you and I.

Counting the beats,
Counting the slow heart beats,
The bleeding to death of time in slow heart beats,
Wakeful they lie.

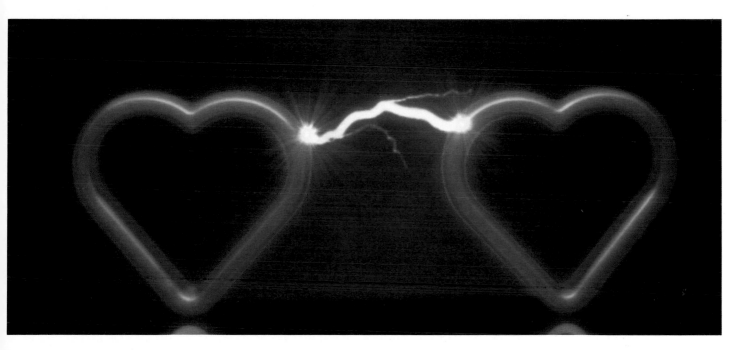

Electric Love by Steve Martin. 1985. Neon

LAY YOUR SLEEPING HEAD, MY LOVE

W. H. Auden

Lay your sleeping head, my love,
Human on my faithless arm;
Time and fevers burn away
Individual beauty from
Thoughtful children, and the grave
Proves the child ephemeral:
But in my arms till break of day
Let the living creature lie,
Mortal, guilty, but to me
The entirely beautiful.

Soul and body have no bounds:
To lovers as they lie upon
Her tolerant enchanted slope
In their ordinary swoon,
Grave the vision Venus sends
Of supernatural sympathy,
Universal love and hope;
While an abstract insight wakes
Among the glaciers and rocks
The hermit's sensual ecstasy.

Certainty, fidelity
On the stroke of midnight pass
Like vibrations of a bell
And fashionable madmen raise
Their pedantic boring cry;
Every farthing of the cost,
All the dreaded cards foretell,
Shall be paid, but from this night
Not a whisper, not a thought,
Not a kiss nor look be lost.

Beauty, midnight, vision dies:
Let the winds of dawn that blow
Softly round your dreaming head
Such a day of sweetness show
Eye and knocking heart may bless,
Find the mortal world enough;
Noons of dryness see you fed
By the involuntary powers,
Nights of insult let you pass
Watched by every human love.

Forgiveness by Gilbert + George. 1982. 95 x 79". Courtesy Sonnabend Gallery, New York

THE SISTERS
Roy Campbell

After hot loveless nights, when cold winds stream
Sprinkling the frost and dew, before the light,
Bored with the foolish things that girls must dream
Because their beds are empty of delight,

Two sisters rise and strip. Out from the night
Their horses run to their low-whistled pleas—
Vast phantom shapes with eyeballs rolling white,
That sneeze a fiery steam about their knees:

Through the crisp manes their stealthy prowling hands,
Stronger than curbs, in slow caresses rove,
They gallop down across the milk-white sands
And wade far out into the sleeping cove:

The frost stings sweetly with a burning kiss
As intimate as love, as cold as death:
Their lips, whereon delicious tremors hiss
Fume with the ghostly pollen of their breath.

Far out on the grey silence of the flood
They watch the dawn in smouldering gyres expand
Beyond them: and the day burns through their blood
Like a white candle through a shuttered hand.

Women Running on the Beach by Pablo Picasso. 1922. Oil on plywood, 13⅜ x 16¾". Musée Picasso, Paris

THE ISLAND
ON SUNDAY AFTERNOONS

Mary Ann Larkin

In those photos of my mother
and her friends on Neville Island
beside that old mill town
there was something
that hinted at a betrayal
Although they were young
and pleased with themselves
dressed in Sunday greys and browns
a touch of lace and fur
arms around each other
one knew
that life would not unroll brightly for them

    In the pictures
they cling to each other
looking straight at me
their bravery
caught in a half–light
trapped by some web
of darkness or inaction

My mother loved Sis Aaron best
They are always next to each other
their arms entwined
Sis was round and blonde
with blue eyes
my mother tall and dark
Sis Aaron and her children
used to come at Christmas
We played poker in the dining room
while Mother and Sis sat in the living room
murmuring to each other
I always wanted to know what they talked about

what best friends said to each other
when they grew up
but they sat in our living room
as they'd sat on the island
a stillness between them
looking just so
at the noisy children
the shadowy men

For surely, they felt it to be the best part
Queen Anne's lace and the goldenrod
in the fall
young men walking out
in their Sunday suits
the walk home in the waiting dusk
as if they knew
this was to be their share
arms entwined
heading back over the bridge
into the grey houses
smelling of cigars
men asleep on horsehair sofas
waiting mothers rocking

My mother took me to Sis's funeral
She had waited to die
until her son came home from the Army
Before my mother died
I came upon her moaning
        on her bed

Now I study the old photos
try to puzzle it out—
whether a curse from the mills,
or from some chant muttered at the birth
of beauty in that grey city where
soot blotted out the sun . . .

Love (Pittsburgh, 1955–1956). Gelatin silver print by Eugene Smith.
Courtesy of the Center for Creative Photography/Black Star

Untitled by Keith Haring. 1985. Lithograph

LOVE ONE ANOTHER

FROM *The Prophet*

Kahlil Gibran

Love one another, but make not a bond of love:

Let it rather be a moving sea between the shores of your souls.

Fill each other's cup but drink not from one cup.

Give one another of your bread but eat not from the same loaf.

Sing and dance together and be joyous, but let each one of you be alone.

Even as the strings of a lute are alone though they quiver with the same music.

Give your hearts, but not into each other's keeping.

For only the hand of Life can contain your hearts.

And stand together yet not too near together:

For the pillars of the temple stand apart,

And the oak tree and the cypress grow not in each other's shadow.

KISSING

Brian Mueller

Kissing someone on the lips
is like sharing a ripe fruit
while dancing in the snow
you try to devour them until sparks
fly and you spin in a circle
and you fall and you feel
like you fell in the ocean. She
whispers in your ear "I love
you."

Heart and Hand Valentine by unknown artist.
Possibly Connecticut, 1840–60.
Cut paper, varnish, and ink, 14 x 12".
Collection of the Museum of American
Folk Art, New York;
Museum of American Folk Art purchase.
1981.12.15

SOFT, TO YOUR PLACES

Thomas Kinsella

Soft, to your places, animals,
Your legendary duty calls.
    It is, to be
Lucky for my love and me.
    And yet we have seen that all's
A fiction that is heard of love's difficulty.

And what if the simple primrose show
That mighty work went on below
    Before it grew
A moral miracle for us two?
    Since of ourselves we know
Beauty to be an easy thing, this will do.

But O when beauty's brought to pass
Will Time set down his hour-glass
    And rest content,
His hand upon that monument?
    Unless it is so, alas
That the heart's calling is but to go stripped and diffident.

Soft, to your places, love; I kiss
Because it is, because it is.

TOUCH

Octavio Paz

TRANSLATED FROM SPANISH BY CHARLES TOMLINSON

My hands
Open the curtains of your being
Clothe you in a further nudity
Uncover the bodies of your body
My hands
Invent another body for your body

Goat and Woman by Pauline Bewick. 1978.
Watercolor on handmade paper, 22¾ x 31½".
In the Collection of the Arbutus Lodge Hotel, Cork, Ireland

62

MOCK ORANGE

Louise Glück

It is not the moon, I tell you.
It is these flowers
lighting the yard.

I hate them.
I hate them as I hate sex,
the man's mouth
sealing my mouth, the man's
paralyzing body—

And the cry that always escapes,
the low, humiliating
premise of union—

In my mind tonight
I hear the question and pursuing
    answer
fused in one sound
that mounts and mounts and
    then
is split into the old selves,
the tired antagonisms. Do you
    see?
We were made fools of.
And the scent of mock orange
drifts through the window.

How can I rest?
How can I be content
when there is still
that odor in the world?

Rape of Proserpine (detail) by Gian Lorenzo Bernini. 1621–22. Marble,
height 8' 4⅜". Galleria Borghese, Rome

I KNEW A WOMAN

Theodore Roethke

I knew a woman, lovely in her bones,
When small birds sighed, she would sigh back at them;
Ah, when she moved, she moved more ways than one:
The shapes a bright container can contain!
Of her choice virtues only gods should speak,
Or English poets who grew up on Greek
(I'd rather have them sing in chorus, cheek to cheek).

How well her wishes went! She stroked my chin,
She taught me Turn, and Counter-turn, and Stand;
She taught me Touch, that undulant white skin;
I nibbled meekly from her proffered hand;
She was the sickle; I, poor I, the rake,
Coming behind her for her pretty sake
(But what prodigious mowing we did make).

Love likes a gander, and adores a goose:
Her full lips pursed, the errant note to seize;
She played it quick, she played it light and loose;
My eyes, they dazzled at her flowing knees;
Her several parts could keep a pure repose,
Or one hip quiver with a mobile nose
(She moved in circles, and those circles moved).

Let seed be grass, and grass turn into hay:
I'm martyr to a motion not my own:
What's freedom for? To know eternity.
I swear she cast a shadow white as stone.
But who would count eternity in days?
These old bones live to learn her wanton ways:
(I measure time by how a body sways).

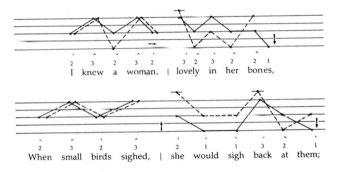

I Knew a Woman, from *Patterns of Poetry:
An Encyclopedia of Forms* by Miller Williams.
Reprinted by permission of Louisiana State University Press

Interior with Plant, Reflection Listening by Lucian Freud.
1967–68. Oil on canvas, 48 x 48". Private Collection

THIS BODY THAT YOU LOVE SO MUCH

Barbara Angell

This body that you love so much
will take its turn,
abandoned briefcase,
lost papers, old
sack of news.

You love its fires, its ears,
and how it moves, it moves,
this body
that you love so much.

It wants sun,
daylight, feet
moving. Music.
Not to be skull
or star.

It hangs on so,
old suit of bones,
on its way to
the final room,
last speck, look
of sun or dust,

this body,
its feathers,
old stems and pieces,
what you could give away.

Your dreams, where
they go: become
a fragment of some story,
an edge of afternoon
in another city.

Then you are wind
maybe, a shimmering
in winter, as of
a spool winding

as you begin
hopefully
the long turn
toward light.

TO MY DEAR AND LOVING HUSBAND

Anne Bradstreet

If ever two were one, then surely we.
If ever man were lov'd by wife, then thee.
If ever wife was happy in a man,
Compare with me, ye women, if you can.
I prize thy love more than whole mines of gold,
Or all the riches that the East doth hold.
My love is such that rivers cannot quench,
Nor aught but love from thee give recompense.
Thy love is such I can no way repay;
The heavens reward thee manifold I pray.
Then while we live, in love let's so persevere,
That when we live no more, we may live ever.

The Kiss by Gustav Klimt. 1907–8. Oil on canvas, 70⅞ x 72". Osterreichische Galerie, Vienna

A Canton Junk, from *Illustrations of China and Its People* by John Thomson. 1873. Photography Collection, The New York Public Library

THE RIVER-MERCHANT'S WIFE: A LETTER

Rihaku (Li T'ai Po)

TRANSLATED FROM CHINESE BY EZRA POUND

While my hair was still cut straight across my forehead
I played about the front gate, pulling flowers.
You came by on bamboo stilts, playing horse,
You walked about my seat, playing with blue plums.
And we went on living in the village of Chōkan:
Two small people, without dislike or suspicion.

At fourteen I married My Lord you.
I never laughed, being bashful.
Lowering my head, I looked at the wall.
Called to, a thousand times, I never looked back.

At fifteen I stopped scowling,
I desired my dust to be mingled with yours
Forever and forever and forever.
Why should I climb the look out?

At sixteen you departed,
You went into far Ku-tō-en, by the river of swirling eddies,
And you have been gone for five months.
The monkeys make sorrowful noise overhead.

You dragged your feet when you went out.
By the gate now, the moss is grown, the different mosses,
Too deep to clear them away!
The leaves fall early this autumn, in wind.
The paired butterflies are already yellow with August
Over the grass in the West garden;
They hurt me. I grow older.
If you are coming down through the narrows of the river Kiang,
Please let me know beforehand,
And I will come out to meet you
        As far as Chō-fū-Sa.

Big Moon Face and *Cityscape* by Red Grooms.
Both constructions dated 1962, used in
Shoot the Moon 16–mm film. Respectively 42 x 52 x 18"
and 38¼ x 71 x 11". Both Collection Saskia Grooms,
New York

LETTER TO NEW YORK

Elizabeth Bishop

In your next letter I wish you'd say
Where you are going and what you are doing:
How are the plays, and after the plays,
What other pleasures you're pursuing.

Taking cabs in the middle of the night,
Driving as if to save your soul
Where the road goes round and round the park
And the meter glares like a moral owl.

And the trees look so queer and green
Standing alone in big black caves,
And suddenly you're in a different place
Where everything seems to happen in waves.

And most of the jokes you just can't catch,
Like dirty words rubbed off a slate,
And the songs are loud but somewhat dim
And it gets so terribly late.

And coming out of the brownstone houses
To the gray sidewalk, the watered street,
One side of the buildings rise with the sun
Like a glistening field of wheat.

Wheat, not oats, dear. I'm afraid
If it's wheat, it's none of your sowing.
Nevertheless I'd like to know
What you are doing and where you are going.

WEDDING DAY
Seamus Heaney

I am afraid.
Sound has stopped in the day
And the images reel over
And over. Why all those tears,

The wild grief on his face
Outside the taxi? The sap
Of mourning rises
In our waving guests.

You sing behind the tall cake
Like a deserted bride
Who persists, demented,
And goes through the ritual.

When I went to the Gents
There was a skewered heart
And a legend of love. Let me
Sleep on your breast to the airport.

TWO HUSBANDS
Henry Taylor

1
She says she'll leave him if he screws around;
why not attempt it, if that's all it takes?
He fears forgiveness; through her, he has found
uprightness in his dreams of dodged mistakes.

2
The youthful urge to kill has left him dry,
that filled their first years with ecstatic woe;
he is content to wait, and watch things die:
as life goes on, he learns to let it go.

A DEDICATION TO MY WIFE

T. S. Eliot

To whom I owe the leaping delight
That quickens my senses in our wakingtime
And the rhythm that governs the repose of our sleepingtime,
    The breathing in unison

Of lovers whose bodies smell of each other
Who think the same thoughts without need of speech
And babble the same speech without need of meaning.

No peevish winter wind shall chill
No sullen tropic sun shall wither
The roses in the rose-garden which is ours and ours only

But this dedication is for others to read:
These are private words addressed to you in public.

T. S. Eliot. Photograph by E. O. Hoppé.
November 1919. Courtesy the Mansell Collection

THE AUTHOR TO HIS WIFE,
OF A WOMAN'S ELOQUENCE

Sir John Harington

My Mall, I mark that when you mean to prove me
To buy a velvet gown, or some rich border,
Thou call'st me good sweet heart, thou swear'st to love me,
Thy locks, thy lips, thy looks, speak all in order,
Thou think'st, and right thou think'st, that these do move me,
That all these severally thy suit do further:
    But shall I tell thee what most thy suit advances?
    Thy fair smooth words? no, no, thy fair smooth haunches.

Sidelong Glance. Photograph by Robert Doisneau. 1948

TO JUDITH ASLEEP

John Ciardi

My dear, darkened in sleep, turn from the moon
That riots on curtain-stir with every breeze
Leaping in moths of light across your back . . .
Far off, then soft and sudden as petals shower
Down from wired roses—silently, all at once—
You turn, abandoned and naked, all let down
In ferny streams of sleep and petaled thighs
Ripping into my flesh's buzzing garden.

Far and familiar your body's myth-map lights,
Traveled by moon and dapple. Sagas were curved
Like scimitars to your hips. The raiders' ships
All sailed to your one port. And watchfires burned
Your image on the hills. Sweetly you drown
Male centuries in your chiaroscuro tide
Of breast and breath. And all my memory's shores
You frighten perfectly, washed familiar and far.

Ritual wars have climbed your shadowed flank
Where bravos dreaming of fair women tore
Rock out of rock to have your cities down
In loot of hearths and trophies of desire.

And desert monks have fought your image back
In a hysteria of mad skeletons.
Bravo and monk (the heads and tails of love)
I stand, a spinning coin of wish and dread,

Counting our life, our chairs, our books and walls,
Our clock whose radium eye and insect voice
Owns all our light and shade, and your white shell
Spiraled in moonlight on the bed's white beach;
Thinking, I might press you to my ear
And all your coils fall out in sounds of surf
Washing away our chairs, our books and walls,
Our bed and wish, our ticking light and dark.

Child, child, and making legend of my wish
Fastened alive into your naked sprawl—
Stir once to stop my fear and miser's panic
That time shall have you last and legendry
Undress to old bones from its moon brocade.
Yet sleep and keep our prime of time alive
Before that death of legend. My dear of all

Saga and century, sleep in familiar-far.
Time still must tick *this is, I am, we are.*

Reclining Nude by Amedeo Modigliani. c. 1919. Oil on canvas, 28½ x 45⅞". Collection, The Museum of Modern Art, New York. Mrs. Simon Guggenheim Fund

THE FUNERAL OF MARTIN LUTHER KING, JR.

Nikki Giovanni

His headstone said
FREE AT LAST, FREE AT LAST
But death is a slave's freedom
We seek the freedom of free men
And the construction of a world
Where Martin Luther King could have lived and
    preached non-violence

Atlanta
4–9–'68

Evening (Melancholy: On the Beach) by Edvard Munch. 1896. Woodcut, printed in color, 16¼ x 18".
Collection, The Museum of Modern Art, New York. Abby Aldrich Rockefeller Fund

IN RAINY SEPTEMBER

Robert Bly

In rainy September, when leaves grow down to the dark,
I put my forehead down to the damp, seaweed-smelling sand.
The time has come. I have put off choosing for years,
perhaps whole lives. The fern has no choice but to live;
for this crime it receives earth, water, and night.

We close the door. "I have no claim on you."
Dusk comes. "The love I have had with you is enough."
We know we could live apart from one another.
The sheldrake floats apart from the flock.
The oaktree puts out leaves alone on the lonely hillside.

Men and women before us have accomplished this.
I would see you, and you me, once a year.
We would be two kernels, and not be planted.
We stay in the room, door closed, lights out.
I weep with you without shame and without honor.

FOR MY LOVER,
RETURNING TO HIS WIFE

Anne Sexton

She is all there.
She was melted carefully down for you
and cast up from your childhood,
cast up from your one hundred favorite aggies.

She has always been there, my darling.
She is, in fact, exquisite.
Fireworks in the dull middle of February
and as real as a cast-iron pot.

Let's face it, I have been momentary.
A luxury. A bright red sloop in the harbor.
My hair rising like smoke from the car window.
Littleneck clams out of season.

She is more than that. She is your have to have,
has grown you your practical your tropical growth.
This is not an experiment. She is all harmony.
She sees to oars and oarlocks for the dinghy,

has placed wild flowers at the window at breakfast,
sat by the potter's wheel at midday,
set forth three children under the moon,
three cherubs drawn by Michelangelo,

done this with her legs spread out
in the terrible months in the chapel.
If you glance up, the children are there
like delicate balloons resting on the ceiling.

She has also carried each one down the hall
after supper, their heads privately bent,
two legs protesting, person to person,
her face flushed with a song and their little sleep.

I give you back your heart.
I give you permission—

for the fuse inside her, throbbing
angrily in the dirt, for the bitch in her
and the burying of her wound—
for the burying of her small red wound alive—

for the pale flickering flare under her ribs,
for the drunken sailor who waits in her
    left pulse,
for the mother's knee, for the stockings,
for the garter belt, for the call—

the curious call
when you will burrow in arms and breasts
and tug at the orange ribbon in her hair
and answer the call, the curious call.

She is so naked and singular.
She is the sum of yourself and your dream.
Climb her like a monument, step after step.
She is solid.

As for me, I am a watercolor.
I wash off.

Melancholy by Edgar Degas, c. 1874. Oil on canvas, 7½ x 9¾″. The Phillips Collection, Washington, D.C.

LOVE IN THE PLURAL

Mukula Kadima–Nzuji

neither this sobbing ocean
in the moon of your swelling voice
nor the milky vapour
on the window of my waking
nor this flood of men
in the margin of my shadow
which yearns for a safe shelter
nor the slipstreams on camelback
in the desert of my solitude
nor the spindrift nor the seaweeds
pillows for my storm–filled head
are able to decipher
where I inspect myself in vain
the reverse side of mirrors.

Face Mask. African, Zaire, Songye, 19th–20th century.
Wood and paint, height 17½". The Metropolitan Museum of Art.
The Michael C. Rockefeller Memorial Collection, Bequest of
Nelson A. Rockefeller, 1979 (1979.206.83)

I LOVED YOU, EVEN NOW I MAY CONFESS

Alexander Pushkin

TRANSLATED FROM RUSSIAN BY REGINALD MAINWARING HEWITT

I loved you, even now I may confess,
   Some embers of my love their fire retain;
But do not let it cause you more distress,
   I do not want to sadden you again.
Hopeless and tonguetied, yet I loved you dearly
   With pangs the jealous and the timid know;
So tenderly I loved you, so sincerely,
   I pray God grant another love you so.

MEN LOVED WHOLLY BEYOND WISDOM

Louise Bogan

Men loved wholly beyond wisdom
Have the staff without the banner.
Like a fire in a dry thicket,
Rising within women's eyes
Is the love men must return.
Heart, so subtle now, and trembling,
What a marvel to be wise,
To love never in this manner!
To be quiet in the fern
Like a thing gone dead and still,
Listening to the prisoned cricket
Shake its terrible, dissembling
Music in the granite hill.

Bazille and Camille by Claude Monet. 1865.
Oil on canvas, 36⅝ x 27⅛". National Gallery of Art,
Washington, Ailsa Mellon Bruce Collection

Sylvia Plath, London, 1959. Photograph © Rollie McKenna

THE RIVAL

Sylvia Plath

If the moon smiled, she would resemble you.
You leave the same impression
Of something beautiful, but annihilating.
Both of you are great light borrowers.
Her O–mouth grieves at the world; yours is unaffected,

And your first gift is making stone out of everything.
I wake to a mausoleum; you are here,
Ticking your fingers on the marble table, looking for cigarettes,
Spiteful as a woman, but not so nervous,
And dying to say something unanswerable.

The moon, too, abases her subjects,
But in the daytime she is ridiculous.
Your dissatisfactions, on the other hand,
Arrive through the mailslot with loving regularity,
White and blank, expansive as carbon monoxide.

No day is safe from news of you,
Walking about in Africa maybe, but thinking of me.

Black Triangle with White by Ellsworth Kelly. 1977.
Collage and ink on paper, 31½ x 34½".
Collection of Whitney Museum
of American Art, New York.
Purchase with funds
from Philip Morris,
Incorporated

DRAWING THE TRIANGLE

Charles Simic

I reserve the triangle
For the wee hours,
The chigger-sized hours.

I like how it starts out
And never gets there.
I like how it starts out.

In the meantime, the bedroom window
Reflecting the owlish aspect
Of the face and the interior.

One hopes for tangents
Surreptitiously in attendance
Despite the rigors of the absolute.

AND WOULD IT HAVE BEEN WORTH IT?
FROM "The Love Song of J. Alfred Prufrock"

T. S. Eliot

And would it have been worth it, after all,
Would it have been worth while,
After the sunsets and the dooryards and the sprinkled streets,
After the novels, after the teacups, after the skirts that trail along the floor—
And this, and so much more?—
It is impossible to say just what I mean!
But as if a magic lantern threw the nerves in patterns on a screen:
Would it have been worth while
If one, settling a pillow or throwing off a shawl,
And turning toward the window, should say:
    "That is not it at all,
    That is not what I meant, at all."

After the Meeting by Cecilia Beaux. 1914.
Oil on canvas, 40^{15}/$_{16}$ x 28^{1}/$_{8}$".
The Toledo Museum of Art, Ohio;
Gift of Florence Scott Libbey

Eakins' Students at the Site for "The Swimming Hole." Albumen print by Thomas Eakins. 1883. 6½ x 4¾".
The J. Paul Getty Museum, Malibu, California

TWENTY-EIGHT YOUNG MEN BATHE BY THE SHORE

Walt Whitman

Twenty-eight young men bathe by the shore,
Twenty-eight young men and all so friendly;
Twenty-eight years of womanly life and all so lonesome.

She owns the fine house by the rise of the bank,
She hides, handsome and richly drest aft the blinds of the window.

Which of the young men does she like the best?
Ah the homeliest of them is beautiful to her.

Where are you off to, lady? for I see you,
You splash in the water there, yet stay stock still in your room.

Dancing and laughing along the beach came the twenty-ninth bather,
The rest did not see her, but she saw them and loved them.

The beards of the young men glisten'd with wet, it ran from their long hair,
Little streams pass'd all over their bodies.

An unseen hand also pass'd over their bodies,
It descended tremblingly from their temples and ribs.

The young men float on their backs, their white bellies bulge to the sun,
They do not ask who seizes fast to them.

They do not know who puffs and declines with pendant and bending arch,
They do not think whom they souse with spray.

The Sea Nymph (from the *Odysseus Collages*) by Romare Bearden.
1977. Collage on board, 44 x 32".
Private Collection, Scarsdale, New York

NOCTURNE OF THE WHARVES
Arna Bontemps

All night they whine upon their ropes and
    boom
against the dock with helpless prows:
these little ships that are too worn for sailing
front the wharf but do not rest at all.
Tugging at the dim gray wharf they think
no doubt of China and of bright Bombay,
and they remember islands of the East,
Formosa and the mountains of Japan.
They think of cities ruined by the sea
and they are restless, sleeping at the wharf.

Tugging at the dim gray wharf they think
no less of Africa. An east wind blows
and salt spray sweeps the unattended decks.
Shouts of dead men break upon the night.
The captain calls his crew and they respond—
the little ships are dreaming—land is near.
But mist comes up to dim the copper coast,
mist dissembles images of the trees.
The captain and his men alike are lost
and their shouts go down in the rising sound
    of waves.

Ah little ships, I know your weariness!
I know the sea-green shadows of your dream.
For I have loved the cities of the sea,
and desolations of the old days I
have loved: I was a wanderer like you
and I have broken down before the wind.

Are You Jealous? by Paul Gauguin. 1892. Oil on canvas, 26 x 35". Pushkin Museum of Fine Arts, Moscow

THE DANGER OF LOSS
Robert Bly

On a clear day, the jealous
Are jealous of ash leaves,
Flies, all jewelry of air.
They sit, gloating,
And grumpy with rage,
Under their blowing hair.

But the kind pine, though
Heavenless, does not drop
Green tears on earth.
And partnerships of sheep
Walk half asleep
On the mountains of death.

But a man may lose the jewel
On earth because
Of wife or job;
For what he saves
He cares nothing, and goes
Sullenly to a deep grave.

LIGHT BREAKS WHERE NO SUN SHINES

Dylan Thomas

Light breaks where no sun shines;
Where no sea runs, the waters of the heart
Push in their tides;
And, broken ghosts with glow-worms in their heads,
The things of light
File through the flesh where no flesh decks the bones.

A candle in the thighs
Warms youth and seed and burns the seeds of age;
Where no seed stirs,
The fruit of man unwrinkled in the stars,
Bright as a fig;
Where no wax is, the candle shows its hairs.

Dawn breaks behind the eyes;
From poles of skull and toes the windy blood
Slides like a sea;
Nor fenced, nor staked, the gushers of the sky
Spout to the rod
Divining in a smile the oil of tears.

Night in the sockets rounds,
Like some pitch moon, the limit of the globes;
Day lights the bone;
Where no cold is, the skinning gales unpin
The winter's robes;
The film of spring is hanging from the lids.

Light breaks on secret lots,
On tips of thoughts where thoughts smell in the rain;
When logics die,
The secret of the soil grows through the eye,
And blood jumps in the sun;
Above the waste allotments the dawn halts.

INTERLUDE

Mary Ann Larkin

Will death take me as sweetly
Will I moan and go willingly
become for the last time a layer of dark

But afterwards, no sun
will slide down the closet door
across my grandmother's quilt—
its torn panes
no longer hiding
the quilt beneath
We will take no soapy bath
you, dreaming of breakfast
when I will slice your noon potatoes
into the darkening onions

I picture a field going on
light and shadow like today
only we won't care
Or will we give anything
just to feel
a drop from the frying pan
pop, against our skin

O love,
we will have no skin

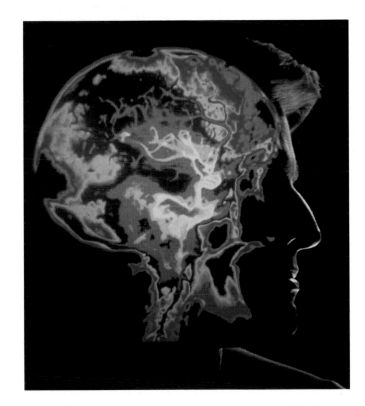

Man's Profile Superimposed on Color–Coded Angiogram of His Brain.
Photograph by Howard Sochurek. c. 1973

LIFE FOR MY CHILD IS SIMPLE, AND IS GOOD
FROM "The Womanhood"

Gwendolyn Brooks

Life for my child is simple, and is good.
He knows his wish. Yes, but that is not all.
Because I know mine too.
And we both want joy of undeep and unabiding things,
Like kicking over a chair or throwing blocks out of a window
Or tipping over an icebox pan
Or snatching down curtains or fingering an electric outlet
Or a journey or a friend or an illegal kiss.
No. There is more to it than that.
It is that he has never been afraid.
Rather, he reaches out and lo the chair falls with a beautiful crash,
And the blocks fall, down on the people's heads,
And the water comes slooshing sloppily out across the floor.
And so forth.
Not that success, for him, is sure, infallible.
But never has he been afraid to reach.
His lesions are legion.
But reaching is his rule.

The Street by Jacob Lawrence. 1957. Casein on paper, 32¼ x 24".
Private Collection, Terry Dintenfass Gallery

MORNING SONG

Sylvia Plath

Love set you going like a fat gold watch.
The midwife slapped your footsoles, and your bald cry
Took its place among the elements.

Our voices echo, magnify your arrival. New statue.
In a drafty museum, your nakedness
Shadows our safety. We stand round blankly as walls.

I'm no more your mother
Than the cloud that distils a mirror to reflect its own slow
Effacement at the wind's hand.

All night your moth-breath
Flickers among the flat pink roses. I wake to listen:
A far sea moves in my ear.

One cry, and I stumble from bed, cow-heavy and floral
In my Victorian nightgown.
Your mouth opens clean as a cat's. The window square

Whitens and swallows its dull stars. And now you try
Your handful of notes;
The clear vowels rise like balloons.

Family Group by Henry Moore. 1948–49. Bronze (cast 1950), 59¼ x 46½ x 29⅞", including base.
Collection, The Museum of Modern Art, New York. A. Conger Goodyear Fund

MY SON, MY EXECUTIONER

Donald Hall

My son, my executioner,
   I take you in my arms,
Quiet and small and just astir,
   And whom my body warms.

Sweet death, small son, our instrument
   Of immortality,
Your cries and hungers document
   Our bodily decay.

We twenty-five and twenty-two,
   Who seemed to live forever,
Observe enduring life in you
   And start to die together.

I take into my arms the death
   Maturity exacts,
And name with my imperfect breath
   The mortal paradox.

Lady Bug by Pamela T. Creighton. 1963.
Poster paints and oil-based pastels, 14 x 20".
Collection of Margaret Stuart Hunter

LADY BUG

Anonymous

Lady bug, lady bug,
Fly away home,
Your house is on fire,
Your children will burn.

WHO ARE YOU, LITTLE I

e. e. cummings

who are you,little i

(five or six years old)
peering from some high

window;at the gold

of november sunset

(and feeling:that if day
has to become night

this is a beautiful way)

Child at a Window by Edouard Vuillard. 1901. Oil on cardboard,
13⁹⁄₁₆ x 10¹⁄₁₆". Courtesy of Dumbarton Oaks Research Library
and Collection, Washington, D.C.

Canoe of Fate by Roy De Forest. 1974. Polymer on canvas, 66¾ x 90¼".
Philadelphia Museum of Art: Adele Haas Turner and Beatrice Pastorius Turner Fund

FURNITURE

Phyllis Harris

there are youngsters now
younger than I, moving as nomads
through the makeshift camping grounds

who do not hope for what was
expected: the catalog comforts
of minor success

nor do they imagine
changelessness, that what they encounter
remains

whose parents
in the suburbs, in the small
midwestern towns

have set down heavy houses on the land
& filled them
with a weight of furnishings, & in a manner
held them down

but not their children: who dreamed of Indians
tracking.
& move lightly, from city
to city

exchanging
adornments; themselves the only
shelter they have found

The Lamb, from *Songs of Innocence and Experience* by William Blake.
1789–94. Relief etching with watercolor.
Reproduced by permission of The Huntington Library,
San Marino, California

THE TIGER
William Blake

Tiger, tiger, burning bright
In the forests of the night,
What immortal hand or eye
Could frame thy fearful symmetry?

In what distant deeps or skies
Burnt the fire of thine eyes?
On what wings dare he aspire?
What the hand dare seize the fire?

And what shoulder and what art
Could twist the sinews of thy heart?
And, when thy heart began to beat,
What dread hand and what dread feet?

What the hammer? What the chain?
In what furnace was thy brain?
What the anvil? What dread grasp
Dare its deadly terrors clasp?

When the stars threw down their spears,
And water'd heaven with their tears,
Did He smile His work to see?
Did He who made the lamb make thee?

Tiger, tiger, burning bright
In the forests of the night,
What immortal hand or eye
Dare frame thy fearful symmetry?

Calvin and Hobbes by Bill Watterson. © 1990 Universal Press Syndicate. Reprinted with permission. All rights reserved

SONNET

Elizabeth Bishop

I am in need of music that would flow
Over my fretful, feeling finger-tips,
Over my bitter, tainted, trembling lips,
With melody, deep, clear, and liquid-slow.
Oh, for the healing swaying, old and low,
Of some song sung to rest the tired head,
And over quivering limbs, dream flushed to glow!

There is a magic made by melody.
A spell of rest, and quiet breath, and cool
Heart, that sinks through fading colors deep
To the subaqueous stillness of the sea,
And floats forever in a moon-green pool,
Held in the arms of rhythm and of sleep.

Music by Henri Matisse. 1939. Oil on canvas,
45⅛ x 45⅜". Albright-Knox Art Gallery,
Buffalo, New York. Room of Contemporary Art Fund, 1940

The Horse by Alexander Calder. 1928.
Walnut, 15½ x 34¾ x 8⅛".
Collection, The Museum of Modern Art,
New York. Acquired through
the Lillie P. Bliss Bequest

YOU AIN'T NOTHIN'
BUT A HOUND DOG

FROM "Hound Dog"
Song lyrics by Jerry Leiber and Mike Stoller

You ain't nothin' but a Hound Dog,
    cryin' all the time.
You ain't nothin' but a Hound Dog,
    cryin' all the time.
Well, you ain't never caught a rabbit
    and you ain't no friend of mine.

Elvis Presley's Birthday, Graceland—1960; Memphis, Tennessee.
Photograph © Henri Dauman

A BIRTH

James Dickey

Inventing a story with grass,
I find a young horse deep inside it.
I cannot nail wires around him;
My fence posts fail to be solid,

And he is free, strangely, without me.
With his head still browsing the greenness,
He walks slowly out of the pasture
To enter the sun of his story.

My mind freed of its own creature,
I find myself deep in my life
In a room with my child and my mother,
When I feel the sun climbing my shoulder

Change, to include a new horse.

111

Mrs. Edith Mahon by Thomas Eakins. 1904.
Oil on canvas, 20 x 16".
Smith College Museum of Art,
Northampton, Massachusetts.
Purchased 1931

PORTRAIT: MY WIFE

John Holmes

"I'd rather be loved, and love, than be Shakespeare."
Ambition is what calls the mountain till it comes,
Or goes where it is and gnaws the mountain down.
But she is not ambitious. She makes a choice,
Which, being she, is foregoing neither wholly,
As: how should she not be of the many-parted poet
Miranda sometimes, Lear's daughter, or Elizabeth,
Or not be as she is, fresh beauty to the use?
She writes; is a woman; Shakespeare would know
 her.

As for the other, loving her makes me that poet.
Once I desired her, not seeing who she was,
Having been then married to her a morning's years,
To the straight smooth back, the opening kiss,
The laughter a red peony thrown and bursting.

She is my stranger every day. She is wretched
With doubt; everyone seeks her reassurance;
Quick-tempered as firecrackers, scornful, clean;
A spiritual materialist, Eve with clothes on.
No one knows her loneliness or believes it;
Not I, but that it is the edge of my world,
And when she comes back, then I can come
 back
From looking over. She is warm, her cheek
 is warm.
Bored with sameness, we re-read one another.
We break up housekeeping to keep our house
 alive,
And are thought a steady pair. Oh, she has her
 wish!
She, whatever she does next, is my one wish.

PORTRAIT

Edna St. Vincent Millay

Over and over I have heard,
As now I hear it,
Your voice harsh and light as the scratching of dry leaves over the hard ground,
Your voice forever assailed and shaken by the wind from the island
Of illustrious living and dead, that never dies down,
And bending at moments under the terrible weight of the perfect word,
Here in this room without fire, without comfort of any kind,
Reading aloud to me immortal page after page conceived in a mortal mind.
Beauty at such moments before me like a wild bright bird
Has been in the room, and eyed me, and let me come near it.

I could not ever nor can I to this day
Acquaint you with the triumph and the sweet rest
These hours have brought to me and always bring,—
Rapture, coloured like the wild bird's neck and wing,
Comfort, softer than the feathers of its breast.
Always, and even now, when I rise to go,
Your eyes blaze out from a face gone wickedly pale;
I try to tell you what I would have you know,—
What peace it was; you cry me down; you scourge me with a salty flail;
You will not have it so.

BUICK
Karl Shapiro

As a sloop with a sweep of immaculate wing on her delicate spine
And a keel as steel as a root that holds in the sea as she leans,
Leaning and laughing, my warm-hearted beauty, you ride, you ride,
You tack on the curves with parabola speed and a kiss of goodbye,
Like a thoroughbred sloop, my new high-spirited spirit, my kiss.

As my foot suggests that you leap in the air with your hips of a girl,
My finger that praises your wheel and announces your voices of song,
Flouncing your skirts, you blueness of joy, you flirt of politeness,
You leap, you intelligence, essence of wheelness with silvery nose,
And your platinum clocks of excitement stir like the hairs of a fern.

But how alien you are from the booming belts of your birth and the smoke
Where you turned on the stinging lathes of Detroit and Lansing at night
And shrieked at the torch in your secret parts and the amorous tests,
But now with your eyes that enter the future of roads you forget;
You are all instinct with your phosphorous glow and your streaking hair.

And now when we stop it is not as the bird from the shell that I leave
Or the leathery pilot who steps from his bird with a sneer of delight,
And not as the ignorant beast do you squat and watch me depart,
But with exquisite breathing you smile, with satisfaction of love,
And I touch you again as you tick in the silence and settle in sleep.

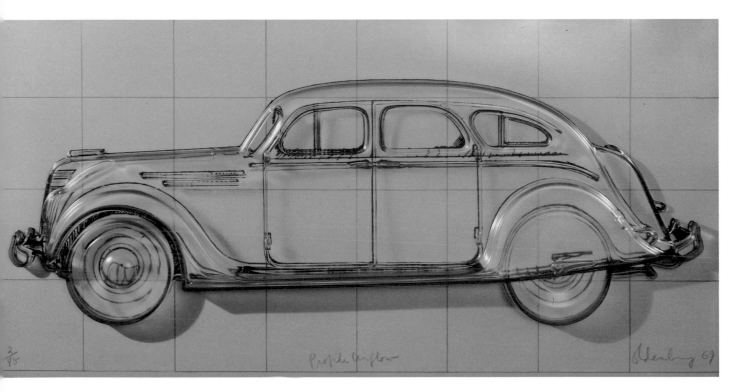

Profile Airflow by Claes Oldenburg. 1968–69. Molded polyurethane over 2-color lithograph (aluminum) on Special Arjomari paper, 33½ x 65½". National Gallery of Art, Washington; Gift of Gemini G.E.L.

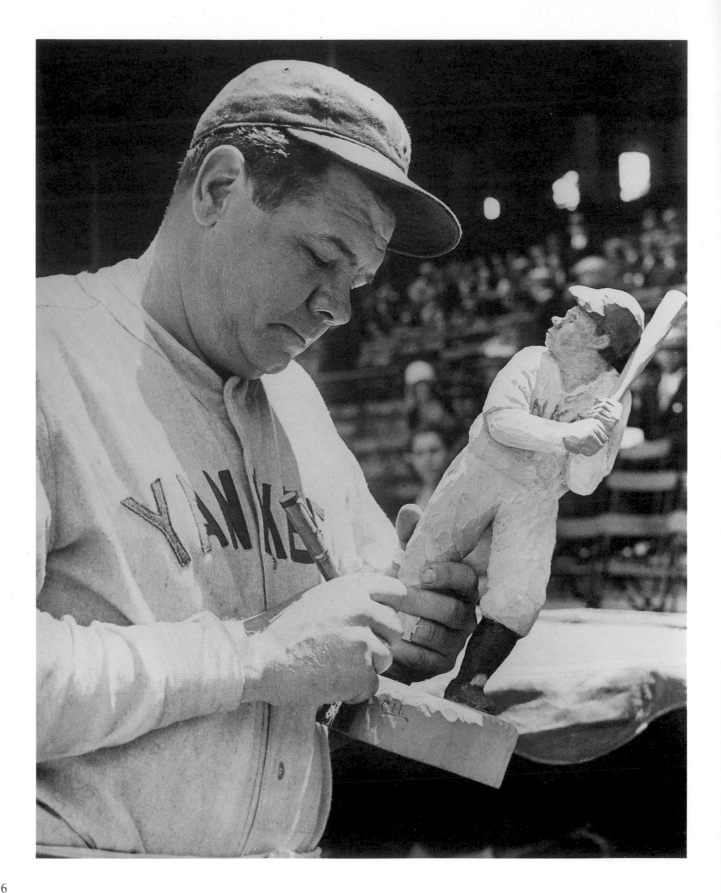

MAYBE FOR LOVE

John Holmes

Set out in an old island garden behind boxwood hedges
Were all the small carved applewood animals to buy,
And I bought three, a hound, a mule, and a wild duck.

Boys and old men last winter under the Carolina ledges
Knifed them out of the hard wood, and I wondered why.
Not for money—they cost so little. Maybe for luck.

The grain of the wood slides all round the small duck
From the bent snaky neck to the fat feathered tail.
But applewood shines the same in hound or mule.

Maybe for love. I thought, yes, maybe the carver, struck
By his own thought of the dog, climbed a fence rail,
Sat, and cut to what wood meant to be, in the cool

Of the mountain evening, looking over the valley, alone.
Hundreds of miles from there, and a long year later,
I stare and rub fondly the mule, the duck, the hound.

Drawn grain of applewood follows the mule's bone,
Hauled back, stubborn. Wood makes the hound a waiter,
A hunter for faint clues but true on the world's ground.

Something wild in an old man's heart I think cut wings
For the wild bird, and for me, for the flying in my mind.
Being stubborn, I bought the mule. I know how I will not.

The hound in my hand searches for me for the next things
I almost have, must have, will send him out to find.
Buying the three, I was the three meanings that I bought.

Babe Ruth Autographing a Carving of Himself.
Photographer unknown. c. 1935.
Collection of Charles Sullivan

IT IS A BEAUTEOUS EVENING, CALM AND FREE

William Wordsworth

It is a beauteous evening, calm and free,
The holy time is quiet as a Nun
Breathless with adoration; the broad sun
Is sinking down in its tranquility;
The gentleness of heaven broods o'er the Sea;
Listen! the mighty Being is awake,
And doth with his eternal motion make
A sound like thunder—everlastingly.
Dear Child! dear Girl! that walkest with me here,
If thou appear untouched by solemn thought,
Thy nature is not therefore less divine:
Thou liest in Abraham's bosom all the year;
And worshipp'st at the Temple's inner shrine,
God being with thee when we know it not.

A Convent Garden, Brittany by William J. Leech. c. 1903.
Oil on canvas, 52 x 42". National Gallery of Ireland, Dublin

Human Face Made from the Words "Allah, Muhammad' Ali, Hasan and Husayn"
Persian calligraphy, 19th century

THE LORD BE PRAISED

Hafiz

TRANSLATED FROM PERSIAN BY PETER AVERY AND JOHN HEATH—STUBBS

The lips of the one I love are my perpetual pleasure:
The Lord be praised, for my heart's desire is attained.

O Fate, cherish my darling close to your breast:
Present now the golden wine–cup, now the rubies of those lips.

They talk scandal about us, and say we are drunks—
The silly old men, the elders lost in their error.

But we have done penance on the pious man's behalf,
And ask God's pardon for what the religious do.

O my dear, how can I speak of being apart from you?
The eyes know a hundred tears, and the soul has a hundred sighs.

I'd not have even an infidel suffer the torment your beauty has caused
To the cypress which envies your body, and the moon that's outshone by your face.

Desire for your lips has stolen from Hafiz' thought
His evening lectionary, and reciting the Book at dawn.

THY RISING IS BEAUTIFUL

From a poem to the sun-god, Aton

Aknaton (Pharaoh Amenhotep IV)

TRANSLATED FROM FOURTEENTH–CENTURY–B.C. EGYPTIAN
BY ANNE AND CHRISTOPHER FREMANTLE

Thy rising is beautiful, O living Aton, lord of Eternity;
Thou art shining, beautiful, strong;
Thy love is great and mighty,
Thy rays are cast into every face.
Thy glowing hue brings life to hearts,
When thou has filled the Two Lands with thy love.
O God who himself fashioned himself,
Maker of every land,
Creator of that which is upon it:
Men, all cattle large and small,
All trees that grow in the soil.
They live when thou dawnest for them,
Thou art the mother and the father of all that thou hast made.

Aknaton (Amenhotep IV). Egyptian, c. 1360 B.C.
Limestone relief, height 3⅛". Staatliche Museen
zu Berlin, Preussischer Kulturbesitz: Ägyptisches Museum

123

ONE'S-SELF I SING

Walt Whitman

One's-self I sing, a simple separate person,
Yet utter the word Democratic, the word En-Masse.

Of physiology from top to toe I sing,
Not physiognomy alone nor brain alone is worthy for the
      Muse, I say the Form complete is worthier far,
The Female equally with the Male I sing.

Of Life immense in passion, pulse, and power,
Cheerful, for freest action form'd under the laws divine,
The Modern Man I sing.

Governor Franklin D. Roosevelt Speaking with Mr. Reuben Appel,
Hyde Park, New York, November 4, 1930.
Photographer unknown

PIED BEAUTY

Gerard Manley Hopkins

Glory be to God for dappled things—
    For skies of couple-colour as a brindled cow;
      For rose-moles all in stipple upon trout
        that swim;
Fresh-firecoal chestnut-falls; finches wings;
    Landscape plotted and pieced—fold, fallow,
      and plough;
      And all trades, their gear and tackle and trim.

All things counter, original, spare, strange,
    Whatever is fickle, freckled (who knows how?)
      With swift, slow; sweet, sour; adazzle, dim;
He fathers-forth whose beauty is past change:
      Praise him.

Self-Portrait by Vincent van Gogh. 1889.
Oil on canvas, 22½ x 17¼ ". From the
Collection of Mrs. John Jay Whitney

Portrait of a Dervish. Indian, early 17th century.
Ink, opaque watercolor, and gold on paper,
8⅝ x 4³⁄₁₆". The Metropolitan Museum of Art,
New York, The Cora Timken Burnett
Collection of Persian Miniatures and Other
Persian Art Objects. Bequest of Cora Timken
Burnett, 1956

MY HEART HAS BECOME CAPABLE
OF EVERY FORM

Ibn al-Arabi
TRANSLATED FROM THIRTEENTH-CENTURY ARABIC
BY ANNE AND CHRISTOPHER FREMANTLE

My heart has become capable of every form: it is a pasture
    for gazelles and a retreat for Christian monks,
And a temple for idols, and the pilgrim's Ka'ba,
    and the tables of the Torah and the book of the Koran.

I follow the religion of Love, whichever way his camels take.
    My religion and my faith is the true religion.

A SUNSET OF THE CITY

Gwendolyn Brooks

(FOR KATHLEEN EILEEN)

Already I am no longer looked at with lechery or love.
My daughters and sons have put me away with marbles and dolls,
Are gone from the house.
My husband and lovers are pleasant or somewhat polite
And night is night.

It is a real chill out,
The genuine thing.
I am not deceived, I do not think it is still summer
Because sun stays and birds continue to sing.

It is summer–gone that I see, it is summer–gone.
The sweet flowers indrying and dying down,
The grasses forgetting their blaze and consenting to brown.

It is a real chill out. The fall crisp comes.
I am aware there is winter to heed.
There is no warm house
That is fitted with my need.

I am cold in this cold house this house
Whose washed echoes are tremulous down lost halls.
I am a woman, and dusty, standing among new affairs.
I am a woman who hurries through her prayers.

Tin intimations of a quiet core to be my
Desert and my dear relief
Come: there shall be such islanding from grief,
And small communion with the master shore.
Twang they. And I incline this ear to tin,
Consult a dual dilemma. Whether to dry
In humming pallor or to leap and die.

Somebody muffed it? Somebody wanted to joke.

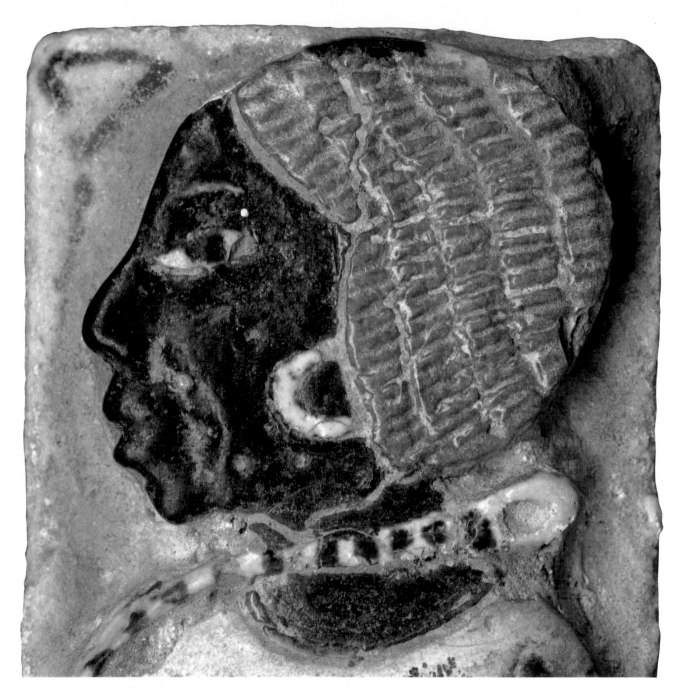

Egyptian Faience Panel Tile with Figure of a Nubian Prisoner (detail), from Temple of Ramses III at Medinet Habu, Thebes. 1182–1151 B.C. (Dynasty 20). 9⅞ x 2⅜". Courtesy, Museum of Fine Arts, Boston. Sears Fund

SOMEWHERE I HAVE NEVER TRAVELLED, GLADLY BEYOND

e. e. cummings

somewhere i have never travelled,gladly beyond
any experience,your eyes have their silence:
in your most frail gesture are things which enclose me,
or which i cannot touch because they are too near

your slightest look easily will unclose me
though i have closed myself as fingers,
you open always petal by petal myself as Spring opens
(touching skilfully,mysteriously)her first rose

or if your wish be to close me,i and
my life will shut very beautifully,suddenly,
as when the heart of this flower imagines
the snow carefully everywhere descending;

nothing which we are to perceive in this world equals
the power of your intense fragility:whose texture
compels me with the colour of its countries,
rendering death and forever with each breathing

(i do not know what it is about you that closes
and opens;only something in me understands
the voice of your eyes is deeper than all roses)
nobody,not even the rain,has such small hands

The Lovers by Pablo Picasso. 1923.
Oil on canvas, 51¼ x 38¼".
National Gallery of Art, Washington;
Chester Dale Collection

THE MIRABEAU BRIDGE

Guillaume Apollinaire

Under the Mirabeau bridge the Seine
   Flows with our loves;
Must I remember once again
Joy followed always after pain?
   Night may come and clock may sound,
   Within your shadow I am bound.

Clasp hand in hand, keep face to face,
   Whilst here below
The bridge formed by our arms' embrace
The waters of our endless longing pass.
   Night may come and clock may sound,
   Within your shadow I am bound.

And like this stream our passions flow,
   Our love goes by;
The violence hope dare not show
Follows time's beat which now falls slow.
   Night may come and clock may sound,
   Within your shadow I am bound.

The days move on; but still we strain
   Back towards time past;
Still to the waters of the Seine
We bend to catch the echo gone.
   Night may come and clock may sound,
   Within your shadow I am bound.

Lovers in the Lilacs by Marc Chagall. 1930.
Oil on canvas, 50½ x 34¾".
Richard S. Zeisler Collection, New York

Yellow Hickory Leaves with Daisy by Georgia O'Keeffe. 1928. Oil on canvas, 30 x 39⅞". The Art Institute of Chicago. Gift of Georgia O'Keeffe to the Alfred Stieglitz Collection, 1965.1180

AND DEATH SHALL HAVE NO DOMINION

Dylan Thomas

And death shall have no dominion.
Dead men naked they shall be one
With the man in the wind and the west moon;
When their bones are picked clean and the clean bones gone,
They shall have stars at elbow and foot;
Though they go mad they shall be sane,
Though they sink through the sea they shall rise again;
Though lovers be lost love shall not;
And death shall have no dominion.

And death shall have no dominion.
Under the windings of the sea
They lying long shall not die windily;
Twisting on racks when sinews give way,
Strapped to a wheel, yet they shall not break;
Faith in their hands shall snap in two,
And the unicorn evils run them through;
Split all ends up they shan't crack;
And death shall have no dominion.

And death shall have no dominion.
No more may gulls cry at their ears
Or waves break loud on the seashores;
Where blew a flower may a flower no more
Lift its head to the blows of the rain;
Though they be mad and dead as nails,
Heads of the characters hammer through daisies;
Break in the sun till the sun breaks down,
And death shall have no dominion.

I TRY TO KEEP

Erica Jong

I try to keep
falling in love
if only to keep
death

at bay.

I know
that the burned
witches,
that the seared flesh
of the enemy—

O we are all
each other's
enemies,
even sometimes those
who lately
were

lovers—

are not
to be reconstituted
nor healed

by my
falling
in love;

& yet
here is
the paradox:

love drives
the poem—

& the poem
is
hope.

Four Marilyns by Andy Warhol. 1962. Acrylic and silkscreen enamel on canvas, 74 x 61".
Courtesy Sonnabend Gallery, New York

Mabel and Alexander Graham Bell.
Photographer unknown. 1903.
The Library of Congress

LAST LOVE

Fyodor Tyutchev

TRANSLATED FROM RUSSIAN BY VLADIMIR NABOKOV

Love at the closing of our days
is apprehensive and very tender.
Glow brighter, brighter, farewell rays
of one last love in its evening splendor.

Blue shade takes half the world away:
through western clouds alone some light
    is slanted.
O tarry, O tarry, declining day,
enchantment, let me stay enchanted.

The blood runs thinner, yet the heart
remains as ever deep and tender.
O last belated love, thou art
a blend of joy and of hopeless surrender.

SHALL I COMPARE THEE
TO A SUMMER'S DAY?

William Shakespeare

Shall I compare thee to a summer's day?
Thou art more lovely and more temperate:
Rough winds do shake the darling buds of May,
And summer's lease hath all too short a date:
Sometime too hot the eye of heaven shines,
And often is his gold complexion dimmed;
And every fair from fair sometime declines,
By chance, or nature's changing course untrimmed;
But thy eternal summer shall not fade,
Nor lose possession of that fair thou owest,
Nor shall death brag thou wanderest in his shade,
When in eternal lines to time thou growest;
    So long as men can breathe, or eyes can see,
    So long lives this, and this gives life to thee.

Autumn Bouquet (Portrait of Vera Repina)
by Ilya Efimovich Repin. 1892.
Oil on canvas, 43¾ x 25⅝".
State Tretiakov Gallery, Moscow

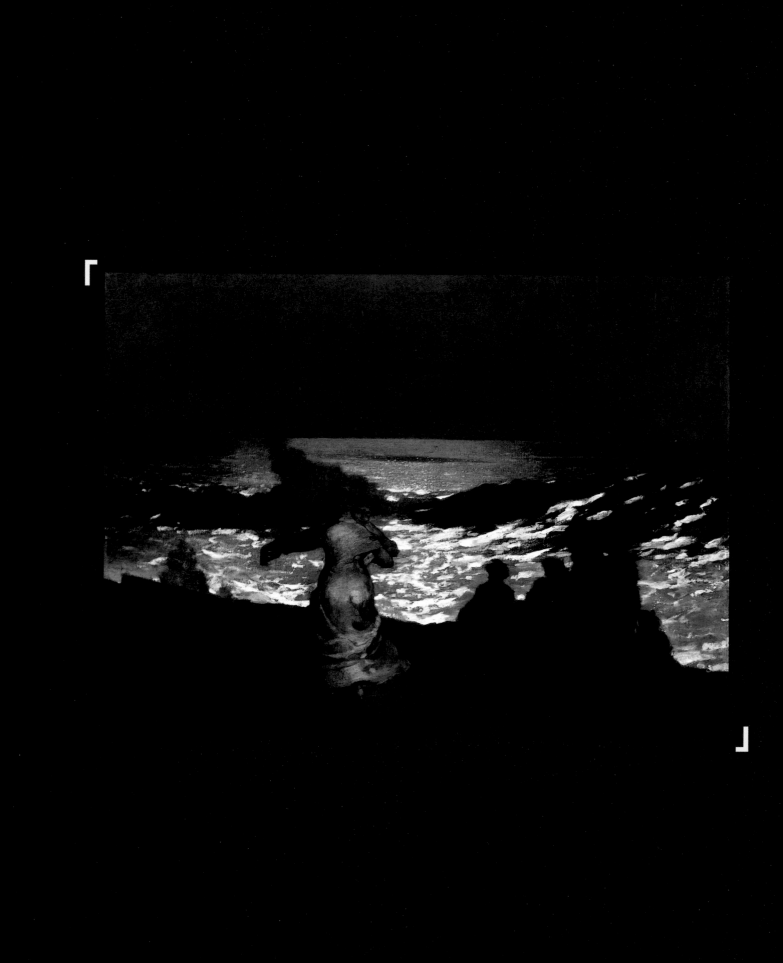

A *Summer Night* by Winslow Homer.
1890. Oil on canvas, 29½ x 39¾".
Musée d'Orsay, Paris

NOW GREEN, NOW BURNING

FROM "TENTH ELEGY. ELEGY IN JOY."
Muriel Rukeyser

Now green, now burning, I make a way for peace.
After the green and long beyond my lake,
among those fields of people, on these illuminated
hills, gold, burnt gold, spilled gold and shadowed blue,
the light of enormous flame, the flowing light of the sea,
where all the lights and nights are reconciled.
The sea at last, where all the waters lead.
And all the wars to this peace.

For the sea does not lie like the death you imagine;
this sea is the real sea, here it is.
This is the living. This peace is the face of the world,
a fierce angel who in one lifetime lives
fighting a lifetime, dying as we all die,
becoming forever, the continual god. . . .

This moment, this seed, this wave of the sea, this look, this instant of love.
Years over wars and an imagining of peace. Or the expiation journey
toward peace which is many wishes flaming together,
fierce pure life, the many–living home.
Love that gives us ourselves, in the world known to all
new techniques for the healing of a wound,
and the unknown world. One life, or the faring stars.

Presence by Mary Frank. 1985–86. Bronze, 28 x 34 x 22".
Photo courtesy Zabriskie Gallery, New York

CHILLS AND FEVER

Charles Sullivan

In and out of time
as time runs out, I twist
and shout the words
I've heard the river sing
when winter lets it go—
I live, I flow—
I'm bringing body heat
to all the secret passages
I know—and as I melt
the frozen melodies I've felt,
what's left of me?

If this is not a dream—
if I am nothing
but a current twisting
through a stream—
then love's no more
or less than chills and fever—
all I feel unreal, and you
imaginary too.
The river floods me suddenly—
cracking the black ice
and sliding past—
if spring is really coming
back at last,
I may not have a month,
a week—in my delirium I seek
the recreation of a season
for a day—an April day that takes me
up through budding woods
and hours to the moment
of our high fields.

There we went from time
to time—in and out
of love as love ran out—
singing songs and telling
stories, ringing bells
with morning glories,
trying to make a right
of many wrongs—remember
how I cried the night
November climbed the hill
behind us? Frost between
the lines we spoke, and death
in every blossom of our breath.

I leave the doors unlocked,
the calendars and clocks
unwound, so then is now
and now I know that nothing
found is lost—my fever breaks,
my body aches for exercise, I stumble
barefoot, coatless down the rows
of silent boats, and what I feel
is what I felt before the music froze—
the loneliness that comes and goes
as time and love run out—again
I shout my crazy song, again I give
those years away, until the river stops
to listen. Only the electric meters
count the cost of living here
in real time.

BIOGRAPHICAL NOTES ON POETS AND ARTISTS

Akhmatova, Anna (Anna Andreyevna Govenko) (1874–1946). Russian writer and translator known for emotionally powerful poetry; *Complete Poems* was published in English in 1990.

Aknaton (Pharaoh Amenhotep IV, also known as Akhenaten). Egyptian ruler, 1365–1347 B.C., who worshiped a sun-god, Aton or Aten, took his name, and wrote poetry in his honor.

Amichai, Yehuda (Born 1924). Poet born in Germany who became an Israeli citizen and soldier; his books in English translations include *Time* (1979) and *Love Poems* (1981).

Angell, Barbara (1930–1990). American writer, teacher, artist whose books include a posthumously published collection of poems, *Turning toward the Light* (1991).

Apollinaire, Guillaume (1880–1918). French writer whose tempestuous life is reflected in such books as *The Poet Assassinated* (English translation, 1968, illustrated by Jim Dine).

Auden, W. H. (1907–1973). Poet and playwright; born in England, became an American citizen in 1946, gave "The Age of Anxiety" its name. Awarded the Pulitzer Prize in 1948.

Bearden, Romare (1911–1988). American artist, best known for his dynamic, brightly colored paintings and collages, whose work appears in many museums and private collections.

Beaux, Cecilia (1855–1942). American artist whose portraits are comparable to those of Sargent and Eakins, but whose fame is not.

Bell, Hugh. Contemporary American photographer and teacher whose subjects range from jazz to business, including some outstanding advertising pictures.

Bernini, Gian Lorenzo (1598–1680). Italian artist who achieved great success as a sculptor and as an architect, in such projects as the interior design and decoration of St. Peter's, Rome.

Bewick, Pauline (Born 1935). Irish artist, prolific in watercolors, whose work often expresses her feeling of being part of the total structure of nature.

Bishop, Elizabeth (1911–1979). American poet, lecturer, who received the Pulitzer Prize in 1956, the National Book Award in 1970, and many other honors.

Blake, William (1757–1827). English poet, artist, mystic, who wrote and illustrated his own books about nature, religion, and other subjects.

Bly, Robert (Born 1926). Prize-winning American poet and translator, more recently recognized as a leader of the men's liberation movement with his prose classic, *Iron John* (1990).

Bogan, Louise (1897–1970). Bollingen Prize–winning American poet whose final collection of poetry, *The Blue Estuaries*, is now in its fifth printing.

Bontemps, Arna (1902–1973). American educator and writer whose poetry is less appreciated than it deserves to be; he also wrote essays about black history and related topics.

Botticelli, Sandro (Alessandro di Mariano) (1445–c. 1510). Florentine painter who captured the human qualities of Medici society before turning to mythological and religious themes, which he also interpreted with humanistic emphasis.

Bradstreet, Anne (c. 1612–1672). English Puritan and American poet who broke through conventions to write from the heart; her husband was governor of the Massachusetts Bay Colony.

Brooks, Gwendolyn (Born 1917). Widely acclaimed and much-loved American poet who won the Pulitzer Prize in 1950; author of *Selected Poems* (1963) and many other books.

Browning, Elizabeth Barrett (1806–1861). English poet who celebrated her love for her husband in sonnets from "the Portuguese," as he affectionately called her.

Browning, Robert (1812–1899). English poet who achieved fame for his dramatic monologues, but is best remembered now for the love poems written to Elizabeth, his wife.

Calder, Alexander (1898–1976). American artist whose highly imaginative works range from delicate jewelry and small animal sculptures to large abstract mobiles and stabiles.

Campbell, Roy (Ignatius Roy Dunnachie) (1902–1957). South African poet who spent many years in Europe and became an accomplished translator of French and Spanish poetry.

Cassatt, Mary (1844–1926). One of the greatest American artists of the Impressionist period, known especially for sensitive paintings and prints of women and children.

Chagall, Marc (1887–1985). Early modern artist, born in Russia, whose work reflects his childhood there as well as the romantic highlights of his later life in France.

Ciardi, John (1916–1986). American poet, editor, and lecturer, whose translations of Dante have won him a lasting place in world literature.

Creighton, Pamela T. (Born 1957). American writer, artist, who began selling her pictures at an unusually early age.

cummings, e. e. (1894–1962). American poet whose unusual, sometimes idiosyncratic verse forms have not completely disguised his depth of feeling and his lyric gifts.

De Forest, Roy (Born 1930). American artist whose colorful paintings combine some of the elements of reality and imagination, old worlds and new.

Degas, Edgar (1834–1917). French artist, best known for lively ballet and racetrack scenes, who was also able to capture the inner life of the individual.

Dickey, James (Born 1923). Prize-winning American poet and novelist, author of *Deliverance* (1970), now Professor of English and poet in residence at the University of South Carolina.

Dickinson, Emily (1830–1886). American poet who lived in seclusion and died unknown, later to gain worldwide recognition as her work was published and appreciated.

Dine, Jim (Born 1935). American painter, sculptor, known for hearts, tools, other series; also author, illustrator of *Welcome Home Lovebirds* (1969) and other books.

Doisneau, Robert (Born 1912). French painter, photographer who drew attention to the small, amusing, often overlooked details of life in Paris.

Donne, John (1572–1631). English writer, clergyman, whose love poetry, mostly unpublished during his lifetime, is distinguished by its intensity of thought and feeling.

Doolittle, Hilda—*see* H. D.

Eakins, Thomas (1844–1916). American artist, photographer, and teacher, whose portraits are prized more for their honesty than for their beauty.

Eliot, T. S. (1888–1965). Outstanding poet, playwright, and critic; born in the United States, became a British citizen in 1927; won the Nobel Prize in 1948.

Elizabeth I (1533–1603). English queen who gave her name to an era but herself (it is said) to no man.

Ensor, James (1860–1949). Belgian Expressionist painter who focused for a time on masks and other features of carnival life.

Finn, David (Born 1921). American photographer, business executive, author of *As the Eye Moves* (1970) and other books, who brings sculptures to life in his photographs.

Frank, Mary (Born 1933). American artist, born in England, whose sculptures and monoprints—especially those of women—are full of movement and feeling.

Freud, Lucian (Born 1922). British artist who goes beyond the limits of conventional portraiture in his attempts to paint his subjects realistically.

Gauguin, Paul (1848–1903). French Post-Impressionist painter who abandoned his family and business career in pursuit of an artistic vision of primitive life in Tahiti and elsewhere.

Gibran, Kahlil (1883–1931). Lebanese philosopher, author of *The Prophet* (1923) and other popular works, whose memory is now honored by a poetry garden in Washington, D.C.

Gilbert (Born 1943) and George (Born 1942). Collaborative British artists whose controversial works include paintings, photographs, videotapes, and themselves as "sculpture."

Giovanni, Nikki (Born 1943). Award-winning American writer, college professor, poetry reader, whose books include *Black Judgment* (1968) and *Those Who Ride the Night Wind* (1983).

Glück, Louise (Born 1943). American poet who teaches at Williams College; books include *Descending Figure* (1980) and *The Triumph of Achilles* (1985).

Graves, Robert (1895–1985). British writer, moved to Majorca; became famous for scholarly work, including historical novels and mythological studies, as well as his own passionate poetry.

Grooms, Red (Born 1937). American artist who uses a wide variety of materials to create objects and environments, such as "Ruckus Rodeo," often with a humorous or satiric effect.

H. D. (Hilda Doolittle) (1886–1961). American "imagist" poet who believed that love could resolve many conflicts; author of *Selected Poems* (1957), *Helen in Egypt* (1961), and other books.

Hafiz (14th cent.). Persian writer whose translated works include *News of Love: Poems of Separation*.

Hall, Donald (Born 1928). American writer, critic, editor, and teacher of poetry; has written *Kicking the Leaves* (1978) and *The Happy Man* (1986), among many other books.

Haring, Keith (1958–1989). American artist whose work was first noticed in streets and subways; his lighthearted "graffiti" evolved into highly prized works of painting and sculpture.

Harington, Sir John (16th cent.). English poet, translator, man of letters, and man of action during the Elizabethan era.

Harris, Phyllis. Contemporary American poet whose work has been published in *The New Yorker* and elsewhere.

Heaney, Seamus (Born 1939). Irish poet, winner of numerous awards, professor at Harvard and Oxford; books include *Station Island* (1984) and *Selected Poems* (1990).

Hilliard, Nicholas (1547–1619). English miniaturist painter, goldsmith, whose patrons included Queen Elizabeth I.

Hockney, David (Born 1937). British artist who moved to the United States; acclaimed for his bold, innovative drawings, paintings, photographic collages, and theatrical set designs.

Holmes, John (1904–1962). American writer, editor, and college professor, whose poetry deserves more recognition than it has received so far.

Homer, Winslow (1836–1910). American magazine illustrator who became a powerful, original artist; his work ranges in subject from the Civil War and the rugged seacoast to scenes of everyday life.

Hopkins, Gerard Manley (1844–1889). English Jesuit, poet who said that his highly original, complex verses "came right" when read aloud.

Hoppé, E. O. (Emil Otto) (1878–1972). German banker who moved to London, became a photographer noted for his natural-looking portraits of well-known people.

Hughes, Ted (né Edward J.) (Born 1930). Winner of many awards, author of many books including *Crow* (1970) and *New Selected Poems* (1982); since 1984 the British Poet Laureate.

Ibn al-Arabi (1165–1240). Muslim theologian and mystic whose life was devoted to seeking universal truths and values that might transcend human differences.

Issahakian, Avedik (1875–1957). Armenian writer, best known for poetry and song lyrics, who spent years in exile because of his political views.

Jacobi, Lotte (Johanna) (1896–1987). Fourth-generation photographer, born in Germany, moved to America, specialized in action pictures of artists and performers.

Jong, Erica (Born 1942). American poet, novelist, teacher, best known for *Fear of Flying* (1973).

Kadima-Nzuji, Mukula. Contemporary poet of Zaire, who helps other French-speaking African writers to gain recognition.

Katz, Alex (Born 1927). American artist whose portraits may simplify the physical features of his subjects in order to reveal more about their character and personality.

Kelly, Ellsworth (Born 1923). American artist who studied and worked in France, later became a leading proponent of "hard-edge" painting.

Kinsella, Thomas (Born 1928). Irish poet, translator, and editor, formerly a civil servant in Dublin, more recently a poetry professor at Temple University, Philadelphia.

Klimt, Gustav (1862–1918). Austrian painter whose work often combines the simplicity of natural beauty with the richness of elaborate ornamentation.

Kokoschka, Oskar (1886–1980). Artist, writer, born in Austria, later a British citizen, best known for his "psychological portraits" and vivid landscapes.

Larkin, Mary Ann (Born 1945). American writer, teacher, and poetry reader, whose books include *The Coil of the Skin* (1982).

Lathrop, Betsy C. American artist who lived in New England during the early 19th century, producing "primitive" paintings in gouache and watercolors.

Lawrence, Jacob (Born 1917). American artist whose distinctive paintings of African-American life are included in many museums and private collections.

Leech, William J. (1881–1968). Irish artist who enjoyed visits to France, producing "impressionistic" sketches as well as more highly finished landscapes and portraits.

Leiber, Jerry. Contemporary American lyricist whose songs have been performed by Elvis Presley and other well-known singers and groups.

Lennon, John Ono (1940–1980). English composer, lyricist, performer, writer, who moved to New York and became an American citizen, but will always be remembered as the leader of The Beatles during the 1960s.

Li T'ai Po—*see* Rihaku.

Linck, Tony (Anthony E.). American photographer who worked on assignments for Time, Inc., and other publishers during the 1930s and 1940s.

McCurry, Steve (Born 1950). American photographer who has won numerous awards for his striking pictures of life in Afghanistan, India, and other exotic places.

McKenna, Rollie (Born 1918). American photographer who succeeded in capturing the changing moods of poets such as Sylvia Plath and Dylan Thomas.

MacLeish, Archibald (1892–1982). Distinguished American man of letters, later Librarian of Congress, who won two Pulitzer Prizes for his poetry.

Madgett, Naomi Long (Born 1923). American poet, college professor, whose books include *Exits and Entrances* (1978) and *Octavia and Other Poems* (1988).

Marlowe, Christopher (1564–1593). English playwright, poet, translator of Latin verse; also involved in the courtly intrigues of his day, and may have been murdered for political reasons.

Martin, Steve. Contemporary American artist who has specialized in creating unusual effects with neon.

Masakaze, Takasaki (20th cent.). Japanese writer whose poems about life and love have the light touch of brushwork in painting.

Matisse, Henri (1869–1954). French artist who achieved strong and colorful effects in various media, including painting, sculpture, stained glass, stencils, and cut paper, despite his failing eyesight.

Michelangelo (di Lodovico Buonarroti Simoni) (1475–1564). Italian Renaissance painter, sculptor, architect, poet, whose great works of art include the ceiling of the Vatican's Sistine Chapel.

Millay, Edna St. Vincent (1892–1950). American poet and playwright, awarded the Pulitzer Prize in 1923, who did much for the cause of women's liberation.

Modigliani, Amedeo (1884–1920). Italian artist who stretched the human figure beautifully out of proportion in sculpture, later in painting.

Monet, Claude (1840–1926). French Impressionist painter whose waterlilies and other natural subjects have made his house and garden at Giverny an international shrine for lovers of art.

Moore, Henry (1898–1986). British artist whose massive, abstract sculptures of people and animals are rooted in his lifelong study of their realistic forms.

Mounicq, Jean (Born 1931). Self-taught French photographer whose dramatic pictures include landscapes, industrial scenes, architecture, and character studies of people.

Mueller, Brian (Born c. 1974). A sixth-grade student in California when his poem "Kissing" was selected for publication in a statewide anthology.

Munch, Edvard (1863–1944). Norwegian painter, graphic artist, best known for haunting pictures such as *The Scream* (1893) and *Anguish* (1894).

Neruda, Pablo (Ricardo Eliecer Neftali Reyes y Basoalto) (1904–1973). Chilean poet and diplomat, won the Nobel Prize in 1973; books include *One Hundred Love Poems* (English translation, 1986).

O'Keeffe, Georgia (1887–1986). Outstanding American artist whose sensuous paintings of deserts, flowers, and other natural subjects are increasingly popular today.

Oldenburg, Claes (Born 1929). American pop artist, best known for whimsical soft sculptures (such as a giant cheeseburger) and outdoor monuments (such as an abstract mouse).

Ono, Yoko (Born 1933). Artist, writer, performer, born in Japan, moved to America, became a citizen, recorded some highly successful albums including *Two Virgins* (1968) and *Double Fantasy* (1980) with John Lennon.

Paz, Octavio (Born 1914). Mexican writer, editor, diplomat, professor, whose widely read books in English include *Selected Poems* (1979).

Picabia, Francis (1878–1953). French painter whose shifting interests included Impressionism, Cubism, Dadaism, and other "modern" approaches, in addition to more realistic ones.

Picasso, Pablo (1881–1973). Spanish artist who lived in France but embraced the whole world; his paintings, sculpture, graphics, and ceramics include many innovative and influential works.

Plath, Sylvia (1932–1963). American poet, posthumously awarded the Pulitzer Prize in 1981, whose suicide cut short a tragic life and a profound creative gift.

Pushkin, Alexander (Aleksandr Sergeyevich) (1799–1837). Russian poet, novelist, whose books include the classics *Boris Godunov* and *Eugene Onegin*.

Raleigh (or Ralegh), Sir Walter (c. 1552–1618). English soldier, courtier, explorer of the "New World," who found time to write bittersweet poems about Queen Elizabeth I and other subjects.

Ray, Man (1890–1976). American artist who produced stunning photographs as well as inventive paintings and three-dimensional objects.

Renoir, Pierre-Auguste (1841–1919). French Impressionist painter, sculptor whose "pearly" images of women and children are among his most popular works.

Repin, Ilya Efimovich (1844–1930). Russian artist who loved to paint his daughter Vera and other young people in settings which emphasized their unity with nature.

Rihaku (Li T'ai Po) (8th cent. A.D.). Chinese poet whose sensitive lines about nature and love were translated into English by Ezra Pound.

Rivera, Diego (1886–1957). Mexican artist who created a number of controversial political murals as well as robust nudes and earthy scenes of everyday life.

Rodin, Auguste (1840–1917). French artist who modeled the human figure with unsurpassed skill in world-renowned sculptures such as *The Thinker* (1879–89) and *Monument to Balzac* (1897–98).

Roethke, Theodore (1908–1963). American writer known for lyric poems such as "Love's Progress," who taught at the University of Washington and elsewhere.

Rossetti, Christina (Georgina) (1830–1894). English poet whose stylized allegories and fairy tales are colored by sensual, naturalistic imagery.

Rukeyser, Muriel (1913–1980). American woman of letters, teacher, social activist, who received numerous awards for her books of "elegies" and other poems.

Sexton, Anne (1928–1974). American writer whose posthumously published *Complete Poems* (1981) includes earlier, hard-to-find volumes such as *Live or Die* (1966) and *Love Poems* (1969).

Shakespeare, William (1564–1616). English actor, playwright, poet, whose identity is sometimes disputed but whose talent is usually not.

Shapiro, Karl (Born 1913). American poet, editor, essayist, professor, awarded the Pulitzer Prize in 1945; books include *The Place of Love* (1942) and many others.

Shinoyama, Kishin (Born 1930). Prolific, popular Japanese photographer whose subjects range from exotic nudes to seemingly mundane details of everyday life.

Shulke, Flip (20th cent.). American photographer who has recorded some great moments in the nation's history.

Simic, Charles (Born 1938). American poet, born in Yugoslavia, now teaches at the University of New Hampshire; books include *Unending Blues* (1986).

Smith, W. Eugene (1918–1978). American photographer whose stirring "photographic essays" of World War II and other large-scale subjects are justly famous.

Sochurek, Howard J. (Born 1924). American photographer who has specialized in scientific and journalistic pictures; has also done advertising illustrations and documentary films.

Stoller, Mike (Michael E.) (Born 1933). American composer and songwriter whose credits include Elvis Presley hits and other favorites.

Sullivan, Charles (Born 1933). American writer, editor, educator; poetry books include *The Lover in Winter* (1991) and *A Woman of a Certain Age* (1992).

Taylor, Henry (Born 1942). American poet, creative writing teacher, who won the Pulitzer Prize for *The Flying Change* (1985).

Thomas, Dylan (1914–1953). Welsh writer whose superb poetry was matched by his magnificent reading voice as he celebrated the human struggle to live, love, and create.

Thomson, John (1837–1921). Scottish photographer who traveled widely in search of interesting subjects for documentary pictures of various cultures and subcultures.

Tyutchev, Fyodor (20th cent.). Russian writer whose poems, translated by the novelist Vladimir Nabokov, express the deeply romantic feelings of his people.

Utamaro (1754–1806). Japanese artist best known for clear, colorful prints depicting the lives of women.

van Gogh, Vincent (1853–1890). Dutch artist whose Post-Impressionist paintings of ordinary people and places, once considered worthless, are now almost priceless.

Velázquez, Diego (Rodriguez de Silva) (1599–1660). Spanish artist who painted both religious and secular subjects with unusual vitality and depth.

Vuillard, Edouard (1868–1940). French painter and lithographer whose numerous scenes of home and family life are warm and intimate.

Warhol, Andy (1928–1987). American artist, filmmaker, who attempted and often succeeded in transforming familiar images of objects and people into extraordinary works of art.

Watterson, Bill (William) (Born 1958). American cartoonist who has won several awards for his syndicated comic strip, *Calvin and Hobbes*, since its inception in 1985.

Whistler, James McNeill (1834–1903). Energetic, disputatious American painter who did much to define the state of the art in works he produced while living abroad.

White, Clarence H. (1871–1925). American photographer, teacher, whose pictures include romantic studies of people as well as abstract outdoor scenes.

Whitman, Walt (1819–1892). American writer whose *Leaves of Grass*, published in 1855 and revised often thereafter, set new standards for the subjects and techniques of poetry.

Williams, Miller (Born 1930). American poet, translator, professor, whose many books include a volume of criticism, *How Does a Poem Mean?* (1974), written with John Ciardi.

Wilson, Reg (20th cent.). British photographer whose pictures convey the movement and drama of ballet and other theatrical subjects.

Wordsworth, William (1770–1850). Romantic, philosophical English writer who led his generation back to nature and became Poet Laureate in the process.

Wyatt, Sir Thomas (1503–1543). English soldier, courtier, diplomat, also a poet and translator of some distinction.

Yeats, W. B. (William Butler) (1865–1939). Irish writer whose unsuccessful pursuit of a strong, independent woman, Maud Gonne, moved him to compose some of the world's greatest love poems.

ACKNOWLEDGMENTS

Grateful acknowledgment is made for permission to reproduce the poems, songs, and excerpts from texts by the following writers. All possible care has been taken to trace ownership of every selection included and to make full acknowledgment. If any errors or omissions have occurred, they will be corrected in subsequent editions, provided that notification is sent to the publisher.

Anna Akhmatova, "You Thought I Was That Type," reprinted by permission of Bloodaxe Books Ltd from *Anna Akhmatova: Selected Poems* translated by Richard McKane (Bloodaxe Books, 1989).

Yehuda Amichai, "A Pity—We Were Such a Good Invention" from *Selected Poetry of Yehuda Amichai*. Copyright © 1986 by Chana Bloch and Stephen Mitchell. Reprinted by permission of HarperCollins Publishers.

Barbara Angell, "This Body That You Love So Much," reprinted by permission of Lauren C. Angell.

W. H. Auden, "Lay Your Sleeping Head, My Love" from *W. H. Auden: Collected Poems* by W. H. Auden, ed. by Edward Mendelson. Copyright 1940 and renewed 1968 by W. H. Auden. Reprinted by permission of Random House, Inc.

Elizabeth Bishop, "Letter to New York" and "Sonnet" from *The Complete Poems, 1927–1979* by Elizabeth Bishop. Copyright © 1940, 1968 by Elizabeth Bishop. Copyright © 1979, 1983 by Alice Helen Methfessel. Reprinted by permission of Farrar, Straus and Giroux, Inc.

Robert Bly, "The Danger of Loss" from *Selected Poems* by Robert Bly. Copyright © 1986 by Robert Bly. Reprinted by permission of HarperCollins Publishers.

Robert Bly, "In Rainy September" from *Loving a Woman in Two Worlds* by Robert Bly. Copyright © 1985 by Robert Bly. Used by permission of Doubleday, a division of Bantam Doubleday Dell Publishing Group, Inc.

Louise Bogan, "Men Loved Wholly Beyond Wisdom" from *The Blue Estuaries* by Louise Bogan. Copyright © 1923, 1968 by Louise Bogan. Reprinted by permission of Farrar, Straus and Giroux, Inc., and Ruth Limmer, Literary Executor, Estate of Louise Bogan.

Arna Bontemps, "Nocturne of the Wharves," reprinted by permission of Harold Ober Associates Incorporated. Copyright © 1963 by Arna Bontemps.

Gwendolyn Brooks, "Life for My Child Is Simple, and Is Good" and "A Sunset of the City," reprinted by permission of Gwendolyn Brooks.

Roy Campbell, "The Sisters," reprinted by permission of Faber and Faber Ltd from *Adamastor* by Roy Campbell.

John Ciardi, "To Judith Asleep," from *I Marry You: A Sheaf of Love Poems*, Rutgers University Press, 1958. Copyright John Ciardi. Reprinted by permission of Judith H. Ciardi.

e. e. cummings, "somewhere i have never travelled, gladly beyond" is reprinted from *ViVa*, poems by e. e. cummings, Edited by George James Firmage, by permission of Liveright Publishing Corporation. Copyright 1931, 1959 by e. e. cummings. Copyright © 1979, 1973 by the Trustees for the e. e. cummings Trust. Copyright © 1979, 1973 by George James Firmage.

e. e. cummings, "who are you,little i" is reprinted from *Complete Poems, 1913–1962*, by e. e. cummings, by permission of Liveright Publishing Corporation. Copyright © 1923, 1925, 1931, 1935, 1938, 1939, 1940, 1944, 1945, 1946, 1947, 1948, 1949, 1950, 1951, 1952, 1953, 1954, 1955, 1956, 1957, 1958, 1959, 1960, 1961, 1962 by the Trustees for the e. e. cummings Trust. Copyright © 1961, 1963, 1968 by Marion Morehouse Cummings.

James Dickey, "A Birth," © 1960 by James Dickey. Reprinted from *Poems: 1957–1967* by permission of Wesleyan University Press and University Press of

New England. This poem first appeared in The New Yorker magazine.

Hilda Doolittle, *see* H.D.

T. S. Eliot, "A Dedication to My Wife" from *Collected Poems 1909–1962* by T. S. Eliot, copyright 1936 by Harcourt Brace Jovanovich, Inc., copyright © 1964, 1963 by T. S. Eliot, reprinted by permission of Harcourt Brace Jovanovich, Inc., and Farrar, Straus and Giroux, Inc.

Anne and Christopher Fremantle, translations of "My Heart Has Become Capable of Every Form" by Ibn al-Arabi and "Thy Rising Is Beautiful" by Aknaton, reprinted by permission of Anne Fremantle.

Kahlil Gibran, "Love One Another," excerpt from *The Prophet* by Kahlil Gibran. Copyright 1923 by Kahlil Gibran and renewed 1951 by Administrators C.T.A. of Kahlil Gibran Estate and Mary G. Gibran. Reprinted by permission of Alfred A. Knopf Inc.

Nikki Giovanni, "The Funeral of Martin Luther King, Jr.," from *Black Feeling, Black Talk, Black Judgment*, copyright 1968 by Nikki Giovanni, published by Broadside Press, Detroit. Permission granted by William Morrow and Company, Inc./Publishers, New York.

Louise Glück, "The Mirror," copyright © 1976, 1977, 1978, 1979, 1980 by Louise Glück. From *Descending Figure*, first published by The Ecco Press in 1980. Reprinted by permission.

Louise Glück, "Mock Orange," copyright © 1985 by Louise Glück. From *The Triumph of Achilles*, first published by The Ecco Press in 1985. Reprinted by permission.

Robert Graves, "Counting the Beats" from *Collected Poems 1975* reprinted by permission of A P Watt Limited on behalf of The Trustees of the Robert Graves Copyright Trust.

H.D. (Hilda Doolittle), "At Baia" and "Helen," from

H.D.: *Collected Poems 1912–1944*. Copyright © 1982 by The Estate of Hilda Doolittle. Reprinted by permission of New Directions Publishing Corporation.

Hafiz, "The Lord Be Praised," from *Thirty Poems*, translated by Peter Avery and John Heath-Stubbs, published by John Murray Publishers Ltd.

Donald Hall, "My Son, My Executioner" from *Old and New Poems* by Donald Hall. Copyright © 1990 by Donald Hall. Reprinted by permission of Houghton Mifflin Co.

Phyllis Harris, "Furniture," reprinted by permission; © 1968 The New Yorker Magazine, Inc.

Seamus Heaney, "Wedding Day" from *Poems, 1965–1975* by Seamus Heaney. Copyright © 1980 by Seamus Heaney. Reprinted by permission of Farrar, Straus and Giroux, Inc.

John Holmes, "Portrait: My Wife" from *The Fortune Teller* by John Holmes. Copyright © 1960 by John Holmes. Reprinted by permission of HarperCollins Publishers.

Ted Hughes, "Lovesong" from *New Selected Poems* by Ted Hughes. Copyright © 1971 by Ted Hughes. Reprinted by permission of HarperCollins Publishers.

Avedik Issahakian, "The Mirage," translated by Diana Der Hovanessian, from *Anthology of Armenian Poetry*, copyright © Diana Der Hovanessian and Marzbed Margossian, Translators and Editors, Columbia University Press, 1978.

Erica Jong, "I Try to Keep" from *Ordinary Miracles: New Poems*, Copyright © 1983 Erica Mann Jong, published by New American Library, reprinted by permission of the poet and New American Library, a division of Penguin Books USA Inc.

Mukula Kadima-Nzuji, "Love in the Plural," reprinted by permission of *Présence Africaine*, no. 97, 1976.

Charles Simic, "Drawing the Triangle," from *Charles Simic Selected Poems 1963–83*. Copyright © 1990 by George Braziller. Reprinted by permission of George Braziller, Inc.

Quentin Stevenson, translation of "The Mirabeau Bridge" by Guillaume Apollinaire, from *The Succession*, published by Oxford University Press. Reprinted by permission of David Higham Associates Limited, London.

Mike Stoller, *see* Jerry Leiber.

Henry Taylor, "Two Husbands," reprinted by permission of Louisiana State University Press from *The Flying Change* by Henry Taylor. Copyright © 1985 by Henry Taylor.

Dylan Thomas, "And Death Shall Have No Dominion," "In My Craft or Sullen Art," and "Light Breaks Where No Sun Shines," from Dylan Thomas: *Poems of Dylan Thomas*. Copyright 1939, 1943, 1946 by New Directions Publishing Corporation. Reprinted by permission of New Directions Publishing Corporation.

INDEX OF POEMS

INDEX OF POETS

INDEX OF ARTISTS